MAX LUCADO

LIFE LESSONS *from*

1 & 2 TIMOTHY
AND TITUS

Ageless Wisdom for Young Leaders

PREPARED BY THE LIVINGSTONE CORPORATION

THOMAS NELSON
Since 1798

Published in Nashville, Tennessee, by Thomas Nelson. Thomas Nelson is a registered trademark of HarperCollins Christian Publishing, Inc.

Produced with the assistance of the Livingstone Corporation. Project staff include Jake Barton, Joel Bartlett, Andy Culbertson, Mary Horner Collins, and Will Reaves.

Editor: Neil Wilson

All Scripture quotations, unless otherwise indicated, are taken from The Holy Bible, New International Version®, NIV®. Copyright © 1973, 1978, 1984, 2011 by Biblica, Inc.™ Used by permission. All rights reserved worldwide.

Scripture quotations marked NKJV are taken from the New King James Version®. Copyright © 1982 by Thomas Nelson. Used by permission. All rights reserved.

Scripture quotations marked NLT are taken from the Holy Bible, New Living Translation, copyright © 1996, 2004, 2015 by Tyndale House Foundation. Used by permission of Tyndale House Publishers, Inc., Carol Stream, Illinois 60188. All rights reserved.

Material for the "Inspiration" sections taken from the following books:

And the Angels Were Silent. Copyright © 2004 by Max Lucado. Thomas Nelson, a registered trademark of HarperCollins Christian Publishing, Inc., Nashville, Tennessee.

Anxious for Nothing. Copyright © 2017 by Max Lucado. Thomas Nelson, a registered trademark of HarperCollins Christian Publishing, Inc., Nashville, Tennessee.

He Still Moves Stones. Copyright © 1993 by Max Lucado. Thomas Nelson, a registered trademark of HarperCollins Christian Publishing, Inc., Nashville, Tennessee.

Just Like Jesus. Copyright © 2003 by Max Lucado. Thomas Nelson, a registered trademark of HarperCollins Christian Publishing, Inc., Nashville, Tennessee.

A Love Worth Giving. Copyright © 2002 by Max Lucado. Thomas Nelson, a registered trademark of HarperCollins Christian Publishing, Inc., Nashville, Tennessee.

Next Door Savior. Copyright © 2003 by Max Lucado. Thomas Nelson, a registered trademark of HarperCollins Christian Publishing, Inc., Nashville, Tennessee.

Shaped by God (previously published as *On the Anvil*). © 2001 by Max Lucado. Tyndale House Publishers, Carol Stream, Illinois 60188.

Storm Warning. Copyright © 1992 by Billy Graham. W Publishing Group, a registered trademark of HarperCollins Christian Publishing, Inc., Nashville, Tennessee.

Unshakable Hope. Copyright © 2018 by Max Lucado. Thomas Nelson, a registered trademark of HarperCollins Christian Publishing, Inc., Nashville, Tennessee.

When God Whispers Your Name. Copyright © 1999 by Max Lucado. Thomas Nelson, a registered trademark of HarperCollins Christian Publishing, Inc., Nashville, Tennessee.

You'll Get Through This. Copyright © 2013 by Max Lucado. Thomas Nelson, a registered trademark of HarperCollins Christian Publishing, Inc., Nashville, Tennessee.

Thomas Nelson titles may be purchased in bulk for educational, business, fundraising, or sales promotional use. For information, please e-mail SpecialMarkets@ThomasNelson.com.

ISBN 978-0-310-08656-7

First Printing October 2018 / Printed in the United States of America

CONTENTS

CONTENTS

HOW TO STUDY THE BIBLE

The Bible is a peculiar book. Words crafted in another language. Deeds done in a distant era. Events recorded in a far-off land. Counsel offered to a foreign people. It is a peculiar book.

It's surprising that anyone reads it. It's too old. Some of its writings date back 5,000 years. It's too bizarre. The book speaks of incredible floods, fires, earthquakes, and people with supernatural abilities. It's too radical. The Bible calls for undying devotion to a carpenter who called himself God's Son.

Logic says this book shouldn't survive. Too old, too bizarre, too radical.

The Bible has been banned, burned, scoffed, and ridiculed. Scholars have mocked it as foolish. Kings have branded it as illegal. A thousand times over the grave has been dug and the dirge has begun, but somehow the Bible never stays in the grave. Not only has it survived, but it has also thrived. It is the single most popular book in all of history. It has been the bestselling book in the world for years!

There is no way on earth to explain it. Which perhaps is the only explanation. For the Bible's durability is not found on *earth* but in *heaven*. The millions who have tested its claims and claimed its promises know there is but one answer: the Bible is God's book and God's voice.

As you read it, you would be wise to give some thought to two questions: *What is the purpose of the Bible?* and *How do I study the Bible?* Time spent reflecting on these two issues will greatly enhance your Bible study.

What is the purpose of the Bible?

Let the Bible itself answer that question: *"From infancy you have known the Holy Scriptures, which are able to make you wise for salvation through faith in Christ Jesus"* (2 Timothy 3:15).

The purpose of the Bible? Salvation. God's highest passion is to get his children home. His book, the Bible, describes his plan of salvation. The purpose of the Bible is to proclaim God's plan and passion to save his children.

This is the reason why this book has endured through the centuries. It dares to tackle the toughest questions about life: *Where do I go after I die? Is there a God? What do I do with my fears?* The Bible is the treasure map that leads to God's highest treasure—eternal life.

But how do you study the Bible? Countless copies of Scripture sit unread on bookshelves and nightstands simply because people don't know how to read it. What can you do to make the Bible real in your life?

The clearest answer is found in the words of Jesus: *"Ask and it will be given to you; seek and you will find; knock and the door will be opened to you"* (Matthew 7:7).

The first step in understanding the Bible is asking God to help you. You should read it prayerfully. If anyone understands God's Word, it is because of God and not the reader.

"The Advocate, the Holy Spirit, whom the Father will send in my name, will teach you all things and will remind you of everything I have said to you" (John 14:26).

Before reading the Bible, pray and invite God to speak to you. Don't go to Scripture looking for your idea, but go searching for his.

Not only should you read the Bible prayerfully, but you should also read it carefully. *"Seek and you will find"* is the pledge. The Bible is not a newspaper to be skimmed but rather a mine to be quarried. *"If you look for it as for silver and search for it as for hidden treasure, then you will understand the fear of the LORD and find the knowledge of God"* (Proverbs 2:4–5).

Any worthy find requires effort. The Bible is no exception. To understand the Bible, you don't have to be brilliant, but you must be willing to roll up your sleeves and search.

"Do your best to present yourself to God as one approved, a worker who does not need to be ashamed and who correctly handles the word of truth" (2 Timothy 2:15).

Here's a practical point. Study the Bible a bit at a time. Hunger is not satisfied by eating twenty-one meals in one sitting once a week. The body needs a steady diet to remain strong. So does the soul. When God sent food to his people in the wilderness, he didn't provide loaves already made. Instead, he sent them manna in the shape of *"thin flakes like frost on the ground"* (Exodus 16:14).

God gave manna in limited portions.

God sends spiritual food the same way. He opens the heavens with just enough nutrients for today's hunger. He provides *"a rule for this, a rule for that; a little here, a little there"* (Isaiah 28:10).

Don't be discouraged if your reading reaps a small harvest. Some days a lesser portion is all that is needed. What is important is to search every day for that day's message. A steady diet of God's Word over a lifetime builds a healthy soul and mind.

It's much like the little girl who returned from her first day at school feeling a bit dejected. Her mom asked, "Did you learn anything?"

"Apparently not enough," the girl responded. "I have to go back tomorrow, and the next day, and the next . . . "

Such is the case with learning. And such is the case with Bible study. Understanding comes little by little over a lifetime.

There is a third step in understanding the Bible. After the asking and seeking comes the knocking. After you ask and search, *"knock and the door will be opened to you"* (Matthew 7:7).

To knock is to stand at God's door. To make yourself available. To climb the steps, cross the porch, stand at the doorway, and volunteer. Knocking goes beyond the realm of thinking and into the realm of acting.

To knock is to ask, *What can I do? How can I obey? Where can I go?*

It's one thing to know what to do. It's another to do it. But for those who do it—those who choose to obey—a special reward awaits them.

"Whoever looks intently into the perfect law that gives freedom, and continues in it—not forgetting what they have heard, but doing it—they will be blessed in what they do" (James 1:25).

What a promise. Blessings come to those who do what they read in God's Word! It's the same with medicine. If you only read the label but ignore the pills, it won't help. It's the same with food. If you only read the recipe but never cook, you won't be fed. And it's the same with the Bible. If you only read the words but never obey, you'll never know the joy God has promised.

Ask. Search. Knock. Simple, isn't it? So why don't you give it a try? If you do, you'll see why the Bible is the most remarkable book in history.

INTRODUCTION TO
The Books of
1 and 2 Timothy and Titus

1 TIMOTHY

Watch a small boy follow his dad through the snow. He stretches to step where his dad stepped. Not an easy task. His small legs extend as far as they can so his feet can fall in his father's prints.

The father, seeing what the son is doing, smiles and begins taking shorter steps, so the son can follow.

It's a picture of discipleship.

In our faith we follow in someone's steps. A parent, a teacher, a hero—none of us is the first to walk the trail. All of us have someone we follow. In our faith we leave footprints to guide others. A child, a friend, a recent convert. None should be left to walk the trail alone.

It's the principle of discipleship.

Timothy didn't walk the trail alone. He followed in the steps of Paul, his father in the faith. Paul knew he was following. He also knew the snow was getting deep. So he slowed his pace to help. He penned a letter to Timothy, giving him practical advice on how to lead a church.

As a young minister, Timothy was faced with all sorts of challenges. Step-by-step, Paul patiently instructed him, and in doing so, he instructs us.

A few questions to consider as you read. Who are you following? When you get where you are going, will it be where you intended? Also, what kind of trail are you leaving? If someone follows your steps, will he or she arrive at the right place?

The message of 1 Timothy urges you: Watch your step.

AUTHOR AND DATE

Paul, who persecuted the early church before his life was radically altered by meeting the risen Jesus on the road to Damascus (see Acts 9:1–31). After spending time in Arabia, Syria, and Cilicia (see Galatians 1:17–21), Paul was selected to minister to the Gentile church in Antioch (see Acts 11:22–26). He became a leader in that congregation and gathered a group of co-workers around him, including Timothy and Titus. Paul delegated many responsibilities to these men during his ministry, and they proved to be a great asset to his efforts in establishing Christian communities. It is believed Paul wrote 1 Timothy after being released from his first Roman imprisonment in AD 62 (see Acts 28:11–30), most likely from the region of Macedonia (see 1 Timothy 1:3). At the time, Timothy was ministering in the city of Ephesus.

SITUATION

The city of Ephesus was famous for its temple dedicated to the goddess Artemis (see Acts 19:28–41) and was thus an influential center of pagan worship. This fact, combined with the influx of false teachers in the region, created a formidable challenge for anyone attempting to lead a Christian community in the city. Timothy was no exception, and he needed support and counsel on how to deal with the issues he and the church were facing. In response, Paul penned this first letter to his younger co-worker to encourage him, motivate him to persevere, and offer guidance on to best address certain false teachings that had arisen in the community—such as assumptions about the law and not allowing marriage and certain foods.

KEY THEMES

- Jesus Christ is the center of the gospel.
- The faith held by the church should be manifested in the behavior of the church.
- Church leaders are expected to live above reproach.
- There is accountability among the church body.

KEY VERSE

Fight the good fight of the faith. Take hold of the eternal life to which you were called when you made your good confession in the presence of many witnesses (1 Timothy 6:12).

CONTENTS

2 TIMOTHY

"I have kept the faith" (2 Timothy 4:7).

They have taken everything else. They have taken Paul's freedom—he's locked in a Roman prison. They have taken his possessions—he hasn't even a shawl to keep him warm. They have taken his churches—he will not see them again. They have taken his future—he is sentenced to die.

What do you have left, Paul? What do you have left to show for your life? Had you stayed a Jew in Jerusalem, you'd have a seat of status and a house of retirement. Had you been more compromising, you might have gone unnoticed by the Romans. Had you been less passionate, you might have pastored a church and stayed in one city. But you were too convinced to compromise—too convicted to stay home.

And now, with the verdict rendered and the end in sight, what do you have left?

The old apostle leans forward with eyes twinkling and says, "I have kept the faith."

That was the heart of the apostle. And that is the heart of this epistle. As far as we know, this is the last one he ever wrote. Paul picks up his pen one final time. He knows the end is near. "I am already being poured out like a drink offering," he tells Timothy, his son in the faith (4:6).

But he has no regrets, only counsel—practical, inspirational counsel for young Timothy, who has been left to lead the church in Ephesus. His tenderness for the young minister peeks out from behind every word. "Do your best to present yourself to God as one approved, a worker who does not need to be ashamed and who correctly handles the word of truth" (2:15).

Timothy never had another teacher like Paul. The world has never had another teacher like Paul. He was convinced of two facts—he was once lost but then saved. He spent a lifetime telling every person who would listen.

In the end, it cost him everything. For in the end, all he had was his faith. But in the end, his faith was all he needed.

AUTHOR AND DATE

Paul is believed to have written 2 Timothy several years after composing his first letter to his younger co-worker (c. AD 67). It appears that Timothy was still ministering in Ephesus, while Paul—instead of being able to freely travel through Macedonia—had been confined in a Roman prison. Unlike Paul's first arrest in Rome, where he was able to stay in a rented house and welcome visitors (see Acts 28:30), this time he was "chained like a criminal" (2 Timothy 2:9). Paul realized he would soon be put to death. As a result, his words to Timothy in this letter are more personal and reflective than in most of his other correspondence.

SITUATION

Paul's motivation for writing this second letter to Timothy seems have been due in part to personal reasons. He had been deserted by certain co-workers and "everyone in the province of Asia" (1:15), other ministry associates were away (see 4:10–12), and only Luke remained with him (see 4:11). Paul wanted Timothy to come to him in prison and bring along John Mark, who had been a former ministry associate (see Acts 12:25; 13:5). Paul was also motivated to write to Timothy to compel him to persevere in the midst of new persecutions that had arisen under the reign of the Roman emperor Nero (see 1:8; 2:3). In this way, Paul hoped his letter would also guide and encourage the believers in Ephesus to persevere in their faith.

KEY THEMES

- The gospel of Christ is worthy of our full commitment.
- The Christian life and ministry will be difficult at times—persevere.
- The Word of God is unique and powerful.
- The life of faith we live will find its rewards in the kingdom of God beyond this life.

KEY VERSE

All Scripture is God-breathed and is useful for teaching, rebuking, correcting and training in righteousness (2 Timothy 3:16).

CONTENTS

TITUS

The letter to Titus was the result of two storms. The first was a storm that struck off the coast of Crete and ultimately left Paul stranded with few resources (see Acts 27). The second was a storm of relativism that struck in Crete and left the people there stranded with few values.

"Cretans are always liars, evil brutes, lazy gluttons" (Titus 1:12). The words didn't originate with Paul but might as well have. He used them to summarize the state of affairs on the island.

He had reason to lament. By the time of Paul, the society had a despicable reputation. Greed was god. Schemers were admired. Cheating was wrong only if you got caught. Right and wrong were determined by the situation, and rape was not a crime.

The economy was so bad that boys were sold as mercenaries as young as the age of twelve. Hence, the people were left with few male role models and fewer abiding beliefs.

Paul established the church in the society and sent Titus to "set in order the things that are lacking" (1:5). And since Paul had definite ideas as to what still needed to be done, we are given definite principles of a healthy church.

Strong leadership is the first item. Titus is instructed to select elders and to do so carefully (see 1:4–16). Strong character is the next. Judging from the style of life in Crete, it would have been easy for the Cretan Christians to compromise their convictions. Paul urges them not to. Judging from the style of life in our world, we could do with the same reminder.

By the way, don't miss Paul's eloquent paragraph on grace (see 2:11–14). We're familiar with grace that saves, but grace does much more. It trains us to deny "ungodliness and worldly lusts" and "live soberly, righteously, and godly in the present age" (verse 12).

Something told Paul the Cretans needed such instruction. Something tells me that we do too.

AUTHOR AND DATE

Titus was a trusted associate of Paul and a considerable help in his ministry. When Paul met with the leaders of the Jerusalem church to discuss sharing the gospel with the Gentiles, he took Titus with him (see Galatians 2:1–3). The fact the leaders did not compel Titus, a Gentile, to be circumcised served to vindicate Paul's stand on what was required for the Gentiles to come to faith in Christ (see 2:3–5). Although Titus is not mentioned in the book of Acts, he presumably worked with Paul in Ephesus during his third missionary journey, and he aided Paul in guiding the church in Corinth we issues arose there (see 2 Corinthians 2:12–13; 7:5–6; 8:6). Paul likely wrote the letter from Macedonia c. AD 63. At the time, Titus was ministering in Crete.

SITUATION

The island of Crete is located in the Mediterranean Sea off the coast of modern-day Greece and Turkey. Paul had evidently introduced the gospel to the inhabitants after he and Titus had visited the island, and he had left Titus in charge to organize and establish the church. Unfortunately, at the time the culture in Crete was widely known for its moral decay, which made the task Paul had set for Titus a formidable challenge. As a result, Paul penned this letter to aid his co-worker in putting "in order what was left unfinished" (Titus 1:5), to guide Titus in how to meet opposition, and how to instruct the believers on their faith and conduct.

KEY THEMES

- The leadership of the church should live lives of honor.
- The older members of the church should train the younger members.
- Good works do not earn our salvation, but they are a product of it.

KEY VERSES

In everything set them an example by doing what is good. In your teaching show integrity, seriousness and soundness of speech that cannot be condemned (Titus 2:7–8).

CONTENTS

LESSON ONE

CHRIST'S POWER TO SAVE

This is a faithful saying and worthy of all acceptance, that Christ Jesus came into the world to save sinners, of whom I am chief.
1 TIMOTHY 1:15 NKJV

1

REFLECTION

Think of someone whose life has dramatically changed since he or she became a believer in Jesus. What has been different since he or she encountered Christ? What's the same? What evidence of Christ's power do you see in that person's life?

SITUATION

Paul had founded the church in Ephesus and spent years teaching the congregation. Later, while under imprisonment and restrictions in Rome, he had learned that Ephesus was undergoing upheaval because of false teachers. In response, Paul had sent Timothy to serve as a living reminder to the truth of the gospel that he had shared with the community. In this first portion of Paul's letter to Timothy, the apostle holds up his own example as a testimony to the power of that gospel. He recalls how he had once been a blasphemer, persecutor of the church, and violent man, but because of God's grace was now a faithful (and grateful) servant of Christ.

OBSERVATION

Read 1 Timothy 1:12–20 from the New International
Version or the New King James Version.

NEW INTERNATIONAL VERSION

[12] I thank Christ Jesus our Lord, who has given me strength, that he considered me trustworthy, appointing me to his service. [13] Even though I was once a blasphemer and a persecutor and a violent man, I was shown mercy because I acted in ignorance and unbelief. [14] The grace of our Lord was poured out on me abundantly, along with the faith and love that are in Christ Jesus.

[15] Here is a trustworthy saying that deserves full acceptance: Christ Jesus came into the world to save sinners—of whom I am the worst. [16] But for that very reason I was shown mercy so that in me, the worst of sinners, Christ Jesus might display his immense patience as an example for those who would believe in him and receive eternal life. [17] Now to the King eternal, immortal, invisible, the only God, be honor and glory for ever and ever. Amen.

[18] Timothy, my son, I am giving you this command in keeping with the prophecies once made about you, so that by recalling them you may fight the battle well, [19] holding on to faith and a good conscience, which some have rejected and so have suffered shipwreck with regard to the faith. [20] Among them are Hymenaeus and Alexander, whom I have handed over to Satan to be taught not to blaspheme.

NEW KING JAMES VERSION

[12] And I thank Christ Jesus our Lord who has enabled me, because He counted me faithful, putting me into the ministry, [13] although I was formerly a blasphemer, a persecutor, and an insolent man; but I obtained mercy because I did it ignorantly in unbelief. [14] And the grace of our Lord was exceedingly abundant, with faith and love which are in Christ Jesus. [15] This is a faithful saying and worthy of all acceptance, that Christ Jesus

came into the world to save sinners, of whom I am chief. [16] However, for this reason I obtained mercy, that in me first Jesus Christ might show all longsuffering, as a pattern to those who are going to believe on Him for everlasting life. [17] Now to the King eternal, immortal, invisible, to God who alone is wise, be honor and glory forever and ever. Amen.

[18] This charge I commit to you, son Timothy, according to the prophecies previously made concerning you, that by them you may wage the good warfare, [19] having faith and a good conscience, which some having rejected, concerning the faith have suffered shipwreck, [20] of whom are Hymenaeus and Alexander, whom I delivered to Satan that they may learn not to blaspheme.

EXPLORATION

1. How does Paul describe his situation before encountering Jesus?

2. What had changed in Paul's life as a result of God's mercy?

3. What reason does Paul give as to *why* God had chosen to show this mercy to him?

4. In what ways does God's plan of salvation demonstrate his grace?

5. How does Paul encourage Timothy to "fight the battle well" (verse 18)?

6. What is the result when people (like Hymenaeus and Alexander) refuse to continue in faith?

INSPIRATION

The apostle Paul entered the pages of Scripture as Saul, the self-professed Pharisee of all Pharisees and the most religious man in town. But all his scruples and law keeping hadn't made him a better person. He was bloodthirsty and angry, determined to extinguish anything and everyone Christian.

His attitude began to change on the road to Damascus. That's when Jesus appeared to him in the desert, knocked him off his high horse, and left him sightless for three days. Paul could see only one direction: inward. And what he saw he did not like. He saw a narrow-minded tyrant. During the time of blindness, God gave him a vision that a man named Ananias would restore his sight. So when Ananias did, Paul "got up and was baptized" (Acts 9:18).

Within a few days he was preaching about Christ. Within a few years he was off on his first missionary journey. Within a couple of decades he was writing the letters we still read today, each one of which makes the case for Christ and the cross.

We aren't told when Paul realized the meaning of grace. Was it immediately on the Damascus road? Or gradually during the three-day darkness? Or after Ananias restored his sight? We aren't told. But we know that Paul got grace. Or grace got Paul. Either way, he embraced the improbable offer that God would make us right with him through Jesus Christ. Paul's logic followed a simple outline:

Our debt is enough to sink us.

God loves us too much to leave us.

So God has found a way to save us. . . .

What a gift God has given you. You've won the greatest lottery in the history of humanity, and you didn't even pay for the ticket! Your soul is secure, your salvation guaranteed. Your name is written in the only book that matters. You're only a few sand grains in the hourglass from a tearless, graveless, painless existence.

This is the message of God, the promise of grace. The declaration Paul preached with unwearied enthusiasm: "What we cannot do, God has done. He justifies us by his grace." Grace is entirely God's. God loving. God stooping. God offering. God caring and God carrying. (From *Unshakable Hope* by Max Lucado.)

REACTION

7. What was the "improbable offer" that Paul chose to embrace?

8. Why do people often think God could never love them or accept them?

9. What does Paul's example show about the extent of God's mercy?

10. Why is it important to recognize our own sinfulness before God?

11. What are some ways that Christ demonstrates his power through people?

---

12. Who is one person in your life whom you can tell about Christ's power to save?

LIFE LESSONS

The power of Christ was evident in Paul's conversion and his life. Although Paul was confident in his role as a mentor and model for Timothy (and others), that confidence never flowed from his past or his performance. He always pointed to what Christ had done and what Christ was doing in his life as reasons to "imitate" him. He was honest about his past shortcomings and failures. The way Paul talked about his past gives us a powerful example of the importance of honestly presenting ourselves—flaws and all—when we talk to others about Christ.

DEVOTION

Lord, you are merciful and forgiving. You sacrificed your life to free us from the bondage of sin. Only you have the power to change our sinful hearts and draw us close to you. Remind us of our need for your transforming power and give us grateful hearts for what you have done for us.

JOURNALING

How has knowing Christ transformed your life? What can you do today
to thank him?

FOR FURTHER READING

To complete the books of 1 and 2 Timothy and Titus during this twelve-part study, read 1 Timothy 1:1–20. For more Bible passages on Christ's saving power, read Luke 19:10; John 3:17; Acts 4:12; Romans 5:8–9; Hebrews 9:14; 1 Peter 1:18–19; 1 John 4:14; and Revelation 1:5.

LESSON TWO

PRAYER AND WORSHIP

I urge . . . that petitions, prayers, intercession
and thanksgiving be made for all people—
for kings and all those in authority, that
we may live peaceful and quiet lives.
1 TIMOTHY 2:1–2

REFLECTION

Consider what you like most about the worship service at your church. Think about the parts of the service that draw you into God's presence. What parts of your worship service would you immediately notice if they were left out? Why?

SITUATION

By the time Paul wrote this letter to Timothy, he had already experienced the full breadth of the Roman Empire's legal and prison system. The apostle was aware of the power of Rome, and he countered that power with respect and honor. He knew God was in control of and works through the systems he places in the world—like governments. Paul's call through Timothy for believers to pray for kings is serious business. So are relationships throughout the church.

OBSERVATION

Read 1 Timothy 2:1–15 from the New International
Version or the New King James Version.

NEW INTERNATIONAL VERSION

[1] I urge, then, first of all, that petitions, prayers, intercession and thanksgiving be made for all people— [2] for kings and all those in authority, that we may live peaceful and quiet lives in all godliness and holiness. [3] This is good, and pleases God our Savior, [4] who wants all people to be saved and to come to a knowledge of the truth. [5] For there is one God and one mediator between God and mankind, the man Christ Jesus, [6] who gave himself as a ransom for all people. This has now been witnessed to at the proper time. [7] And for this purpose I was appointed a herald and an apostle—I am telling the truth, I am not lying—and a true and faithful teacher of the Gentiles.

[8] Therefore I want the men everywhere to pray, lifting up holy hands without anger or disputing. [9] I also want the women to dress modestly, with decency and propriety, adorning themselves, not with elaborate hairstyles or gold or pearls or expensive clothes, [10] but with good deeds, appropriate for women who profess to worship God.

[11] A woman should learn in quietness and full submission. [12] I do not permit a woman to teach or to assume authority over a man; she must be quiet. [13] For Adam was formed first, then Eve. [14] And Adam was not the one deceived; it was the woman who was deceived and became a sinner. [15] But women will be saved through childbearing—if they continue in faith, love and holiness with propriety.

NEW KING JAMES VERSION

[1] Therefore I exhort first of all that supplications, prayers, intercessions, and giving of thanks be made for all men, [2] for kings and all who are in authority, that we may lead a quiet and peaceable life in all godliness and reverence. [3] For this is good and acceptable in the sight of God our Savior,

⁴ who desires all men to be saved and to come to the knowledge of the truth. ⁵ For there is one God and one Mediator between God and men, the Man Christ Jesus, ⁶ who gave Himself a ransom for all, to be testified in due time, ⁷ for which I was appointed a preacher and an apostle—I am speaking the truth in Christ and not lying—a teacher of the Gentiles in faith and truth.

⁸ I desire therefore that the men pray everywhere, lifting up holy hands, without wrath and doubting; ⁹ in like manner also, that the women adorn themselves in modest apparel, with propriety and moderation, not with braided hair or gold or pearls or costly clothing, ¹⁰ but, which is proper for women professing godliness, with good works. ¹¹ Let a woman learn in silence with all submission. ¹² And I do not permit a woman to teach or to have authority over a man, but to be in silence. ¹³ For Adam was formed first, then Eve. ¹⁴ And Adam was not deceived, but the woman being deceived, fell into transgression. ¹⁵ Nevertheless she will be saved in childbearing if they continue in faith, love, and holiness, with self-control.

EXPLORATION

1. According to this passage, what kind of behavior pleases God?

2. What elements should characterize the prayers of God's people?

3. What are some ways people can show their respect and love for God?

_____

_____

_____

_____

4. What inappropriate behavior does Paul say believers should avoid?

_____

_____

_____

_____

5. What basic standards is Paul using to address interpersonal and leadership issues?

_____

_____

_____

_____

6. What is wrong with focusing on outward appearances in worship?

_____

_____

_____

INSPIRATION

God doesn't delay. He never places you on hold or tells you to call again later. God loves the sound of your voice. Always. He doesn't hide when you call. He hears your prayers.

For that reason "be anxious for nothing, but in everything by prayer and supplication, with thanksgiving, let your requests be made known to God" (Philippians 4:6).

With this verse the apostle calls us to take action against anxiety. Until this point he has been assuring us of God's character: his sovereignty, mercy, and presence. Now it is our turn to act on this belief. We choose prayer over despair. Peace happens when people pray.

I like the story of the father who was teaching his three-year-old daughter the Lord's Prayer. She would repeat the lines after him. Finally she decided to go solo. He listened with pride as she carefully enunciated each word, right up to the end of the prayer. "Lead us not into temptation," she prayed, "but deliver us from e-mail."

These days that seems like an appropriate request. God calls us to pray about everything. The terms *prayer, supplication,* and *requests* are similar but not identical. Prayer is a general devotion; the word includes worship and adoration. Supplication suggests humility. We are the supplicants in the sense that we make no demands; we simply offer humble requests. A request is exactly that—a specific petition. We tell God exactly what we want. We pray the particulars of our problems.

What Jesus said to the blind man, he says to us: "What do you want me to do for you?" (Luke 18:41). One would think the answer would be obvious. When a sightless man requests Jesus' help, isn't it apparent what he needs? Yet Jesus wanted to hear the man articulate his specific requests. He wants the same from us . . .

This is no endorsement of the demanding, conditional prayer that presumes to tell God what to do and when. Nor do I suggest that the power of prayer resides in chanting the right formula or quoting some secret code. Do not think for a moment that the power of prayer resides in the way we present it. God is not manipulated or impressed by our formulas or eloquence. But he is moved by the sincere request. After all, is he not our Father? As his children we honor him when we tell him exactly what we need. (From *Anxious for Nothing* by Max Lucado.)

REACTION

7. How can you know that God never "places you on hold"? What assurances do you have from the Bible that God always hears your prayers?

8. How would you define the terms *prayer, supplication,* and *requests*?

9. In what ways can practicing "spiritual disciplines"—meditating on the Bible, prayer, worship, serving others—combat selfishness in an individual?

10. Why is it important to pray for those in authority over you? Why do you think Paul stress that this is pleasing to God?

11. What is the connection between peace and praising God? How does an attitude of thankfulness change your perspective on your problems?

_____

_____

_____

12. How will you fight the temptation to focus more on appearances than on God in worship?

_____

_____

_____

_____

LIFE LESSONS

Believers gather together for the wonderful and serious business of being in God's presence. When they become distracted by power struggles or personal agendas, Christ's agenda for the world fades into the background. We are to pray for the world and witness to people. The way we treat others and the way we treat one another will have a huge impact on our effectiveness in sharing the gospel. What God has given us is never just for our self-enjoyment. Every gift can be used to represent the One who gave it. The world is watching.

DEVOTION

Father, you deserve much more than we ever can give, but we ask that you accept our worship and hear our prayers. Align our plans with your purposes through faithful prayer and sincere worship. Expose our selfishness so that we may repent, receive your forgiveness, and grow in our knowledge of you. Draw us to you and increase our faith.

JOURNALING

In light of this passage, what changes do you need to make in your prayer and worship habits?

FOR FURTHER READING

To complete the books of 1 and 2 Timothy and Titus during this twelve-part study, read 1 Timothy 2:1–15. For more Bible passages on prayer and worship, read 1 Chronicles 16:28–29; Psalms 6:9; 95:6; Matthew 21:22; John 4:24; Acts 2:41–47; and Philippians 4:6.

LEADING OTHERS

Moreover [the leader] must have a good testimony among those who are outside, lest he fall into reproach and the snare of the devil.
1 TIMOTHY 3:7 NKJV

REFLECTION

Think of a leader in your church whom you admire. Identify some of the formative experiences, training, or background that you know the person has had. What positive character traits does this leader display?

_____

_____

_____

_____

_____

_____

_____

_____

_____

_____

_____

_____

SITUATION

Part of Timothy's task was to identify and appoint leaders among the believers in Ephesus. With this in mind, Paul provides him with some specific guidelines in the next part of his letter on how to choose the right individuals for the job. These guidelines for elders (or bishops) are not culturally bound and have stood the test of time. They have, in fact, been the standards by which the church has chosen and tested leaders through the centuries since Paul's writing.

OBSERVATION

*Read 1 Timothy 3:1–16 from the New International
Version or the New King James Version.*

NEW INTERNATIONAL VERSION

[1] Here is a trustworthy saying: Whoever aspires to be an overseer desires a noble task. [2] Now the overseer is to be above reproach, faithful to his wife, temperate, self-controlled, respectable, hospitable, able to teach, [3] not given to drunkenness, not violent but gentle, not quarrelsome, not a lover of money. [4] He must manage his own family well and see that his children obey him, and he must do so in a manner worthy of full respect. [5] (If anyone does not know how to manage his own family, how can he take care of God's church?) [6] He must not be a recent convert, or he may become conceited and fall under the same judgment as the devil. [7] He must also have a good reputation with outsiders, so that he will not fall into disgrace and into the devil's trap.

[8] In the same way, deacons are to be worthy of respect, sincere, not indulging in much wine, and not pursuing dishonest gain. [9] They must keep hold of the deep truths of the faith with a clear conscience. [10] They must first be tested; and then if there is nothing against them, let them serve as deacons.

[11] In the same way, the women are to be worthy of respect, not malicious talkers but temperate and trustworthy in everything.

[12] A deacon must be faithful to his wife and must manage his children and his household well. [13] Those who have served well gain an excellent standing and great assurance in their faith in Christ Jesus.

[14] Although I hope to come to you soon, I am writing you these instructions so that, [15] if I am delayed, you will know how people ought to conduct themselves in God's household, which is the church of the living God, the pillar and foundation of the truth. [16] Beyond all question, the mystery from which true godliness springs is great:

He appeared in the flesh,
> was vindicated by the Spirit,
was seen by angels,
> was preached among the nations,
was believed on in the world,
> was taken up in glory.

NEW KING JAMES VERSION

[1] This is a faithful saying: If a man desires the position of a bishop, he desires a good work. [2] A bishop then must be blameless, the husband of one wife, temperate, sober-minded, of good behavior, hospitable, able to teach; [3] not given to wine, not violent, not greedy for money, but gentle, not quarrelsome, not covetous; [4] one who rules his own house well, having his children in submission with all reverence [5] (for if a man does not know how to rule his own house, how will he take care of the church of God?); [6] not a novice, lest being puffed up with pride he fall into the same condemnation as the devil. [7] Moreover he must have a good testimony among those who are outside, lest he fall into reproach and the snare of the devil.

[8] Likewise deacons must be reverent, not double-tongued, not given to much wine, not greedy for money, [9] holding the mystery of the faith with a pure conscience. [10] But let these also first be tested; then let them serve as deacons, being found blameless. [11] Likewise, their wives must be reverent, not slanderers, temperate, faithful in all things. [12] Let deacons be the husbands of one wife, ruling their children and their own houses well. [13] For those who have served well as deacons obtain for themselves a good standing and great boldness in the faith which is in Christ Jesus.

[14] These things I write to you, though I hope to come to you shortly; [15] but if I am delayed, I write so that you may know how you ought to conduct yourself in the house of God, which is the church of the living God, the pillar and ground of the truth. [16] And without controversy great is the mystery of godliness:

God was manifested in the flesh,
Justified in the Spirit,
Seen by angels,
Preached among the Gentiles,
Believed on in the world,
Received up in glory.

EXPLORATION

1. What are some qualifications that Paul outlines in this passage for church leaders?

2. What practices should elders and deacons avoid?

3. Why is it important for church leaders to manage their families well?

4. What is the danger in giving a new believer a position of leadership in the church?

5. Why is it necessary for churches to have high expectations and standards for their leaders?

_____

_____

_____

_____

6. What reason does Paul give for providing these instructions to Timothy (see verses 14–16)?

_____

_____

_____

INSPIRATION

The temperature is in the twenties. The chill factor is single digit. The West Texas wind stings the ears, and frozen grass cracks beneath the step. It is a cold December day. Even the cattle are smart enough to stay in the barn on mornings like this.

Then what am I doing outside? What am I doing standing in a ditch, ankle deep in water, hunkered over a leaking pipe? And, most of all, why aren't the three guys in the truck helping me? Why are they in there while I'm out here? Why are they warm while I'm cold? Why are they dry while I'm wet?

The answer is found in two words: pecking order.

We can thank Norwegian naturalists for the term. They are the ones who studied the barnyard caste system. By counting the number of times chicken give and receive pecks, we can discern a chain of command. The alpha bird does most of the pecking, and the omega bird gets pecked. The rest of the chickens are somewhere in between.

That day in the oil field, our alpha bird was the crew chief. Beneath him was a former foreman, and beneath the foreman, an illegal immigrant. I was the omega bird. College students on Christmas break come in last . . .

I understood the pecking order. You do too. You know the system. Pecking orders are a part of life. And, to an extent, they should be. We need to know who is in charge. Ranking systems can clarify our roles. The problem with pecking orders is not the order. The problem is with the pecking. . . .

God says that love has no place for pecking orders. Jesus won't tolerate such thinking. Such barnyard mentality may fly on the farm but not in his kingdom. . . . Jesus blasts the top birds of the church, those who roost at the top of the spiritual ladder and spread their plumes of robes, titles, jewelry, and choice seats. Jesus won't stand for it.

It's easy to see why. How can I love others if my eyes are only on me? How can I point to God if I'm pointing at me? And, worse still, how can someone see God if I keep fanning my own tail feathers?

Jesus has no room for pecking orders. Love "does not boast, it is not proud" (1 Corinthians 13:4). His solution to man-made caste systems? A change of direction. In a world of upward mobility, choose downward servility. Go down, not up. "In humility value others above yourselves" (Philippians 2:3).

That's what Jesus did. He flip-flopped the pecking order. While others were going up, he was going down. (From *A Love Worth Giving* by Max Lucado.)

REACTION

7. In practical terms, what does it mean to be a *servant leader* in the church?

_____

_____

_____

_____

8. What steps can leaders take to guard against the sins of pride and arrogance?

9. In what way do you think your church could improve the way it chooses leaders?

10. Why do you think some people hesitate to accept leadership positions in the church?

11. How have you benefited from the ministry of your church leaders?

12. In what ways can you encourage a leader in your church this week?

LIFE LESSONS

Always find a place of service within the church. If you are a leader who must identify abilities and skills in others, do your homework. Observe them carefully—not critically. Your primary task is not to find faults but to develop a list of their best qualities. Before you ask someone to lead, be prepared to tell that individual several positive reasons why you have approached him or her. When you are approached by someone in the church and asked to fill a role or take on a duty, consider the opportunity seriously. Seek to discover what that person saw in you that made him or her think you were suited for the job. The answer may allow you to discover how others see your skills or character.

DEVOTION

Thank you, Father, for sending your Son to show us what it means to be a servant. Make us more like Jesus. Keep us from vying for position and power. Help us to grow in holiness and humility. And above all else, keep our eyes focused on you.

JOURNALING

Which of the characteristics that Paul describes do you need to cultivate in your own life? How?

_____

_____

_____

_____

_____

_____

_____

FOR FURTHER READING

To complete the books of 1 and 2 Timothy and Titus during this twelve-part study, read 1 Timothy 3:1–16. For more Bible passages on leadership, read Matthew 20:25–28; Luke 22:24–27; 1 Corinthians 3:1–9; 2 Timothy 2:24–25; and 1 Peter 5:1–6.

LESSON FOUR

BELIEVING THE TRUTH

Reject profane and old wives' fables,
and exercise yourself toward godliness.
For bodily exercise profits a little, but
godliness is profitable for all things.
1 TIMOTHY 4:7–8 NKJV

REFLECTION

Some people believe it is wrong to have questions about their faith. But there is nothing wrong with questioning—as long as we look for the answers in the right place. The Bible is the source of all truth and has withstood the scrutiny of generations. Think of a time when you had questions about your Christian faith. How did you deal with your doubts?

SITUATION

Now that Paul has provided Timothy with some guidelines for choosing leaders within the church, he moves on to address the issue of false teachers in the community. He encourages Timothy to "be a good minister of Christ Jesus" (4:6) by pointing out the error of these teachings and also by living in a godly manner in the sight of the watching believers. Paul wants Timothy to understand the actions and attitudes that mark a life truly committed to Christ.

OBSERVATION

Read 1 Timothy 4:1–16 from the New International Version or the New King James Version.

New International Version

[1] The Spirit clearly says that in later times some will abandon the faith and follow deceiving spirits and things taught by demons. [2] Such teachings come through hypocritical liars, whose consciences have been seared as with a hot iron. [3] They forbid people to marry and order them to abstain from certain foods, which God created to be received with thanksgiving by those who believe and who know the truth. [4] For everything God created is good, and nothing is to be rejected if it is received with thanksgiving, [5] because it is consecrated by the word of God and prayer.

[6] If you point these things out to the brothers and sisters, you will be a good minister of Christ Jesus, nourished on the truths of the faith and of the good teaching that you have followed. [7] Have nothing to do with godless myths and old wives' tales; rather, train yourself to be godly. [8] For physical training is of some value, but godliness has value for all things, holding promise for both the present life and the life to come. [9] This is a trustworthy saying that deserves full acceptance. [10] That is why we labor and strive, because we have put our hope in the living God, who is the Savior of all people, and especially of those who believe.

[11] Command and teach these things. [12] Don't let anyone look down on you because you are young, but set an example for the believers in speech, in conduct, in love, in faith and in purity. [13] Until I come, devote yourself to the public reading of Scripture, to preaching and to teaching. [14] Do not neglect your gift, which was given you through prophecy when the body of elders laid their hands on you.

[15] Be diligent in these matters; give yourself wholly to them, so that everyone may see your progress. [16] Watch your life and doctrine closely. Persevere in them, because if you do, you will save both yourself and your hearers.

New King James Version

[1] Now the Spirit expressly says that in latter times some will depart from the faith, giving heed to deceiving spirits and doctrines of demons, [2] speaking lies in hypocrisy, having their own conscience seared with a hot iron, [3] forbidding to marry, and commanding to abstain from foods which God created to be received with thanksgiving by those who believe and know the truth. [4] For every creature of God is good, and nothing is to be refused if it is received with thanksgiving; [5] for it is sanctified by the word of God and prayer.

[6] If you instruct the brethren in these things, you will be a good minister of Jesus Christ, nourished in the words of faith and of the good doctrine which you have carefully followed. [7] But reject profane and old wives' fables, and exercise yourself toward godliness. [8] For bodily exercise profits a little, but godliness is profitable for all things, having promise of the life that now is and of that which is to come. [9] This is a faithful saying and worthy of all acceptance. [10] For to this end we both labor and suffer reproach, because we trust in the living God, who is the Savior of all men, especially of those who believe. [11] These things command and teach.

[12] Let no one despise your youth, but be an example to the believers in word, in conduct, in love, in spirit, in faith, in purity. [13] Till I come, give attention to reading, to exhortation, to doctrine. [14] Do not neglect the gift that is in you, which was given to you by prophecy with the laying on of the hands of the eldership. [15] Meditate on these things; give yourself entirely to them, that your progress may be evident to all. [16] Take heed to yourself and to the doctrine. Continue in them, for in doing this you will save both yourself and those who hear you.

EXPLORATION

1. What do you think keeps people from believing the truth of the gospel?

_____

_____

_____

2. What threat do false teachers pose to the church?

3. How do true teachers build up the church?

4. What does Paul mean when he instructs Timothy to "train" himself to be godly?

5. How are believers in Christ to set an example for others?

6. What can believers do to protect themselves from false teaching?

INSPIRATION

Jesus' heart was pure. The Savior was adored by thousands, yet content to live a simple life. He was cared for by women (see Luke 8:1–3), yet never accused of lustful thoughts; scorned by his own creation, but willing to forgive them before they even requested his mercy. Peter, who traveled with Jesus for three and a half years, described him as a "lamb without blemish or defect" (1 Peter 1:19). After spending the same amount of time with Jesus, John concluded, "And in him is no sin" (John 3:5).

Jesus' heart was peaceful. The disciples fretted over the need to feed the thousands, but not Jesus. He thanked God for the problem. The disciples shouted for fear in the storm, but not Jesus. He slept through it. Peter drew his sword to fight the soldiers, but not Jesus. He lifted his hand to heal. His heart was at peace. When his disciples abandoned him, did he pout and go home? When Peter denied him, did Jesus lose his temper? When the soldiers spit in his face, did he breathe fire in theirs? Far from it. He was at peace. He forgave them. He refused to be guided by vengeance.

He refused to be guided by anything other than his high call. Jesus' heart was purposeful. Most lives aim at nothing in particular and achieve it. Jesus aimed at one goal—to save humanity from its sin. He could summarize his life with one sentence: "The Son of Man came to seek and to save the lost" (Luke 19:10). Jesus was so focused on his task that he knew when to say, "My hour has not yet come" (John 2:4) and when to say, "It is finished" (John 19:30). But he was not so focused on his goal that he was unpleasant.

Quite the contrary. How pleasant were his thoughts! Children couldn't resist Jesus. He could find beauty in lilies, joy in worship, and possibilities in problems. He would spend days with multitudes of sick people and still feel sorry for them. He spent over three decades wading through the muck and mire of our sin yet still saw enough beauty in us to die for our mistakes. (From *Just Like Jesus* by Max Lucado.)

REACTION

7. How did the way Jesus lived his life, and the example he set, draw people to him?

_____

_____

_____

_____

8. How does the way you live your life reflect the things you truly believe?

_____

_____

_____

_____

9. What kind of questioning can strengthen a person's faith?

_____

_____

_____

_____

10. What are several practices or activities you can list that promote spiritual growth?

_____

_____

_____

11. What are some ways you can further strengthen your Christian beliefs?

_____

_____

_____

_____

12. How can you help someone who you know is questioning his or her beliefs?

_____

_____

_____

LIFE LESSONS

Timothy was a young man whom the apostle Paul expected to _lead_. He had to step up spiritually, but he also had struggles, doubts, and challenges to overcome. In other words, Timothy was a lot like us. Paul's words to him (and us) make it clear that we will be continually stretched as we live for Christ. We will be required to live beyond our human abilities. The degree to which we grow will be related to the degree to which we allow Christ to grow in us. Like Timothy, we need to learn and practice the central discipline of godliness, even as we are pursuing other good practices in life.

DEVOTION

Father, thank you for continually guiding us as we seek to follow you. You have proven your love for us time and time again. Give us the desire to keep striving toward the goal of knowing you better and becoming more like your Son. Confirm our beliefs and strengthen our faith in you.

JOURNALING

What are some ways you are trying to set example for others in speech, conduct, and love?

FOR FURTHER READING

To complete the books of 1 and 2 Timothy and Titus during this twelve-part study, read 1 Timothy 4:1–16. For more Bible passages on believing the truth, read John 14:6–12; 16:12–15; 20:30–31; Galatians 3:2; 1 Thessalonians 4:14; Hebrews 11:6; and 1 John 4:1–6.

MANAGING RELATIONSHIPS

I charge you, in the sight of God and Christ Jesus and the elect angels, to keep these instructions without partiality, and to do nothing out of favoritism.

1 TIMOTHY 5:21

REFLECTION

Relationships come in all forms, shapes, and sizes. We all have people in our lives who are easy to love . . . and others whom are not even easy to simply tolerate. What is the best advice you have heard on resolving conflicts in relationships? How have you applied that to your life?

SITUATION

Paul, having fortified Timothy against false teachers and extolling him to be a good servant of Christ, now moves on to discuss more detailed instructions on how to minister to different groups within the church. He begins with instructions on how to relate to older and younger men and women in the congregation before address a major concern on his heart: care for the widows and others in need. He concludes with practical guidance on how to honor those elders who are fulfilling their duties before God and how to call out those who are falling short.

OBSERVATION

Read 1 Timothy 5:1–21 from the New International Version or the New King James Version.

NEW INTERNATIONAL VERSION

¹ Do not rebuke an older man harshly, but exhort him as if he were your father. Treat younger men as brothers, ² older women as mothers, and younger women as sisters, with absolute purity.

³ Give proper recognition to those widows who are really in need. ⁴ But if a widow has children or grandchildren, these should learn first of all to put their religion into practice by caring for their own family and so repaying their parents and grandparents, for this is pleasing to God. ⁵ The widow who is really in need and left all alone puts her hope in God and continues night and day to pray and to ask God for help. ⁶ But the widow who lives for pleasure is dead even while she lives. ⁷ Give the people these instructions, so that no one may be open to blame. ⁸ Anyone who does not provide for their relatives, and especially for their own household, has denied the faith and is worse than an unbeliever.

⁹ No widow may be put on the list of widows unless she is over sixty, has been faithful to her husband, ¹⁰ and is well known for her good deeds, such as bringing up children, showing hospitality, washing the feet of the Lord's people, helping those in trouble and devoting herself to all kinds of good deeds.

¹¹ As for younger widows, do not put them on such a list. For when their sensual desires overcome their dedication to Christ, they want to marry. ¹² Thus they bring judgment on themselves, because they have broken their first pledge. ¹³ Besides, they get into the habit of being idle and going about from house to house. And not only do they become idlers, but also busybodies who talk nonsense, saying things they ought not to. ¹⁴ So I counsel younger widows to marry, to have children, to manage their homes and to give the enemy no opportunity for slander. ¹⁵ Some have in fact already turned away to follow Satan.

[16] If any woman who is a believer has widows in her care, she should continue to help them and not let the church be burdened with them, so that the church can help those widows who are really in need.

[17] The elders who direct the affairs of the church well are worthy of double honor, especially those whose work is preaching and teaching. [18] For Scripture says, "Do not muzzle an ox while it is treading out the grain," and "The worker deserves his wages." [19] Do not entertain an accusation against an elder unless it is brought by two or three witnesses. [20] But those elders who are sinning you are to reprove before everyone, so that the others may take warning. [21] I charge you, in the sight of God and Christ Jesus and the elect angels, to keep these instructions without partiality, and to do nothing out of favoritism.

NEW KING JAMES VERSION

[1] Do not rebuke an older man, but exhort him as a father, younger men as brothers, [2] older women as mothers, younger women as sisters, with all purity.

[3] Honor widows who are really widows. [4] But if any widow has children or grandchildren, let them first learn to show piety at home and to repay their parents; for this is good and acceptable before God. [5] Now she who is really a widow, and left alone, trusts in God and continues in supplications and prayers night and day. [6] But she who lives in pleasure is dead while she lives. [7] And these things command, that they may be blameless. [8] But if anyone does not provide for his own, and especially for those of his household, he has denied the faith and is worse than an unbeliever.

[9] Do not let a widow under sixty years old be taken into the number, and not unless she has been the wife of one man, [10] well reported for good works: if she has brought up children, if she has lodged strangers, if she has washed the saints' feet, if she has relieved the afflicted, if she has diligently followed every good work.

[11] But refuse the younger widows; for when they have begun to grow wanton against Christ, they desire to marry, [12] having condemnation because they have cast off their first faith. [13] And besides they learn to

be idle, wandering about from house to house, and not only idle but also gossips and busybodies, saying things which they ought not. [14] Therefore I desire that the younger widows marry, bear children, manage the house, give no opportunity to the adversary to speak reproachfully. [15] For some have already turned aside after Satan. [16] If any believing man or woman has widows, let them relieve them, and do not let the church be burdened, that it may relieve those who are really widows.

[17] Let the elders who rule well be counted worthy of double honor, especially those who labor in the word and doctrine. [18] For the Scripture says, "You shall not muzzle an ox while it treads out the grain," and, "The laborer is worthy of his wages." [19] Do not receive an accusation against an elder except from two or three witnesses. [20] Those who are sinning rebuke in the presence of all, that the rest also may fear.

[21] I charge you before God and the Lord Jesus Christ and the elect angels that you observe these things without prejudice, doing nothing with partiality.

EXPLORATION

1. What instructions does Paul provide for treating those who are older than you? How you to treat those who are younger than you?

_____

_____

_____

_____

2. Read Romans 12:9–21 and Colossians 3:12–17. What additional insights do these passages provide on how believers should treat one another?

_____

_____

_____

3. What guidelines should believers follow in caring for those who are in need?

4. What does it mean to properly care for one's household and family?

5. How does Paul say you are to treat the elders and leaders in your church?

6. What instructions does Paul give when an accusation is made against an elder?

INSPIRATION

"Give me a word picture to describe a relative in your life who really bugs you."

I was asking the question of a half-dozen friends sitting around a lunch table. They all gave me one of those what-in-the-world? expressions. So I explained.

"I keep meeting people who can't deal with somebody in their family. Either their mother-in-law is a witch or their uncle is a bum or they have a father who treats them like they were never born." . . .

"Tar baby in Br'er Rabbit," someone responded. Everyone understood the reference except me. I didn't remember the story of Br'er Rabbit. I asked for the short version. Wily Fox played a trick on Br'er Rabbit. The fox made a doll out of tar and stuck it on the side of the road. When Rabbit saw the tar baby, he thought it was a person and stopped to visit.

It was a one-sided conversation. The tar baby's silence bothered the rabbit. He couldn't stand to be next to someone and not communicate with him. So in his frustration he hit the tar baby and stuck to it. He hit the tar baby again with the other hand and, you guessed it, the other hand got stuck.

"That's how we are with difficult relatives," my fable-using friend explained. "We're stuck to someone we can't communicate with." . . .

You've probably got a tar baby in your life, someone you can't talk to and can't walk away from. A mother who whines, an uncle who slurps his soup, or a sister who flaunts her figure. A dad who is still waiting for you to get a real job or a mother-in-law who wonders why her daughter married you.

Tar-baby relationships—stuck together but falling apart. . . .

Why does life get so *relatively* difficult? If we expect anyone to be sensitive to our needs, it is our family members. When we hurt physically, we want our family to respond. When we struggle emotionally, we want our family to know. But sometimes they act like they don't know. Sometimes they act like they don't care. . . .

I can't assure you that your family will ever give you the blessing you seek, but I know God will. Let God give you what your family doesn't. If your earthly father doesn't affirm you, then let your heavenly Father take his place.

How do you do that? By emotionally accepting God as your father. You see, it's one thing to accept him as Lord, another to recognize him as Savior—but it's another matter entirely to accept him as Father.

To recognize God as Lord is to acknowledge that he is sovereign and supreme in the universe. To accept him as Savior is to accept his gift of salvation offered on the cross. To regard him as Father is to go a step further. Ideally, a father is the one in your life who provides and protects. That is exactly what God has done. . . .

God has proven himself as a faithful father. Now it falls to us to be trusting children. Let God give you what your family doesn't. Let him fill the void others have left. (From *He Still Moves Stones* by Max Lucado.)

REACTION

7. Think about some of the "tar-baby" relationships that you have had in your life. How dead you deal with those difficult relationships?

_____

_____

_____

_____

_____

_____

8. Why is it so important to learn how to manage your relationships with other believers?

_____

_____

_____

_____

_____

9. How does caring for your family demonstrate your commitment and love for Christ?

10. How has your relationship with God had an impact on your relationships with others?

11. What is one principle from this passage that could help you relate better with others?

12. How can you apply this principle to one of your relationships this week?

LIFE LESSONS

As we pass through stages of life, our relationships with others will naturally change. These role-based relationships make up a great deal of our lives, and one of the key words we need to define and practice in every kind of relationship is the word *honor*. We don't owe the same honor to all, but to each person we can offer *some* kind of honor. We need to think carefully about *who* we can honor and *how* we can show that honor in our lives today.

DEVOTION

Father, sometimes the difficulties and demands of our relationships can be overwhelming. Help us fulfill our responsibilities to the people you have placed in our lives. Give us the wisdom to deal with conflicts and the strength to cope with disappointments. May we treat others with love and respect by following the practical guidelines in your Word.

JOURNALING

What do others learn about Jesus from the way you treat your friends and relatives?

FOR FURTHER READING

To complete the books of 1 and 2 Timothy and Titus during this twelve-part study, read 1 Timothy 5:1–25. For more Bible passages on relationships, read Psalm 133:1–3; Proverbs 18:24; Ephesians 2:14–22; 1 Thessalonians 5:12–13; Hebrews 13:1–4; 1 Peter 3:1–8; and 1 John 2:9–11; 3:11–18; 4:20–21.

LESSON SIX

FINDING CONTENTMENT

Now godliness with contentment is great gain.
For we brought nothing into this world, and
it is certain we can carry nothing out.
1 TIMOTHY 6:6–7 NKJV

REFLECTION

What brings you the most happiness in life? Don't just give the expected Sunday school answer. This is personal. Avoid describing what you think should bring you happiness or what you would like to bring you happiness. Be open and honest in your answer.

_____

_____

_____

_____

_____

_____

_____

_____

_____

_____

_____

SITUATION

As Paul nears the end of his letter, he once again draws Timothy's attention to the importance of modelling a life of godliness and contentment for those in the church. He calls Timothy to reject false doctrines that do not agree with the sound teaching he has received, resist the temptation of pursuing riches and material gain, and above all "fight the good fight of faith" (6:12). Paul tells Timothy that he has great expectations for his young protégé, and he is eager to see Timothy continue to live out his potential as a man of God.

OBSERVATION

Read 1 Timothy 6:6–19 from the New International Version or the New King James Version.

New International Version

⁶ But godliness with contentment is great gain. ⁷ For we brought nothing into the world, and we can take nothing out of it. ⁸ But if we have food and clothing, we will be content with that. ⁹ Those who want to get rich fall into temptation and a trap and into many foolish and harmful desires that plunge people into ruin and destruction. ¹⁰ For the love of money is a root of all kinds of evil. Some people, eager for money, have wandered from the faith and pierced themselves with many griefs.

¹¹ But you, man of God, flee from all this, and pursue righteousness, godliness, faith, love, endurance and gentleness. ¹² Fight the good fight of the faith. Take hold of the eternal life to which you were called when you made your good confession in the presence of many witnesses. ¹³ In the sight of God, who gives life to everything, and of Christ Jesus, who while testifying before Pontius Pilate made the good confession, I charge you ¹⁴ to keep this command without spot or blame until the appearing of our Lord Jesus Christ, ¹⁵ which God will bring about in his own time—God, the blessed and only Ruler, the King of kings and Lord of lords, ¹⁶ who alone is immortal and who lives in unapproachable light, whom no one has seen or can see. To him be honor and might forever. Amen.

¹⁷ Command those who are rich in this present world not to be arrogant nor to put their hope in wealth, which is so uncertain, but to put their hope in God, who richly provides us with everything for our enjoyment. ¹⁸ Command them to do good, to be rich in good deeds, and to be generous and willing to share. ¹⁹ In this way they will lay up treasure for themselves as a firm foundation for the coming age, so that they may take hold of the life that is truly life.

⁶ Now godliness with contentment is great gain. ⁷ For we brought nothing into this world, and it is certain we can carry nothing out. ⁸ And having food and clothing, with these we shall be content. ⁹ But those who desire to be rich fall into temptation and a snare, and into many foolish and harmful lusts which drown men in destruction and perdition. ¹⁰ For the love of money is a root of all kinds of evil, for which some have strayed from the faith in their greediness, and pierced themselves through with many sorrows.

¹¹ But you, O man of God, flee these things and pursue righteousness, godliness, faith, love, patience, gentleness. ¹² Fight the good fight of faith, lay hold on eternal life, to which you were also called and have confessed the good confession in the presence of many witnesses. ¹³ I urge you in the sight of God who gives life to all things, and before Christ Jesus who witnessed the good confession before Pontius Pilate, ¹⁴ that you keep this commandment without spot, blameless until our Lord Jesus Christ's appearing, ¹⁵ which He will manifest in His own time, He who is the blessed and only Potentate, the King of kings and Lord of lords, ¹⁶ who alone has immortality, dwelling in unapproachable light, whom no man has seen or can see, to whom be honor and everlasting power. Amen.

¹⁷ Command those who are rich in this present age not to be haughty, nor to trust in uncertain riches but in the living God, who gives us richly all things to enjoy. ¹⁸ Let them do good, that they be rich in good works, ready to give, willing to share, ¹⁹ storing up for themselves a good foundation for the time to come, that they may lay hold on eternal life.

EXPLORATION

1. How would you define contentment? How can a person can find true contentment?

_____

_____

_____

_____

2. In what way does serving God and others make a person "rich"?

_____

_____

_____

_____

3. Why is it important to realize that your earthly goods will be worthless in eternity?

_____

_____

_____

_____

_____

4. What are some of the dangers associated with seeking material wealth?

_____

_____

_____

_____

_____

5. How does focusing on the promise of eternal life help a believer to not get encumbered by material gains and the things of this world?

_____

_____

_____

_____

6. Read Proverbs 28:20 and Ecclesiastes 5:12. What additional warnings do these verses provide to those who seek to be rich in material wealth?

_____

_____

_____

_____

INSPIRATION

Satisfied? That is one thing we are not. We are not satisfied.

We push back from the Thanksgiving table and pat our round bellies. "I'm satisfied," we declare. But look at us a few hours later, back in the kitchen picking the meat from the bone.

We wake up after a good night's rest and hop out of bed. We couldn't go back to sleep if someone paid us. We are satisfied—for a while. But look at us a dozen or so hours later, crawling back in the sheets.

We take a vacation of a lifetime. For years we planned. For years we saved. And off we go. We satiate ourselves with sun, fun, and good food. But we are not even on the way home before we dread the end of the trip and begin planning another.

We are not satisfied.

As a child we say, "If only I were a teenager." As a teen we say, "If only I were an adult." As an adult, "If only I were married." As a spouse, "If only I had kids."

As a parent, "If only my kids were grown." In an empty house, "If only the kids would visit." As a retiree in the rocking chair with stiff joints and fading sight, "If only I were a child again."

We are not satisfied. Contentment is a difficult virtue. Why?

Because there is nothing on earth that can satisfy our deepest longing. We long to see God. The leaves of life are rustling with the rumor that we will—and we won't be satisfied until we do. (From *When God Whispers Your Name* by Max Lucado.)

REACTION

7. Why is it so difficult to be content? What are some of the warning signs of discontentment?

8. Why is it so tempting to trust in wealth instead of God?

9. In what ways can a continual desire for more and more destroy a person?

10. How can trusting in your own wealth lead to pride and arrogance?

11. What are some of the benefits of sharing your resources with others?

12. Why do you think God says you should look to him alone to meet your needs?

LIFE LESSONS

If *godliness* describes how much we are like Christ—the degree to which we reflect his actions and character—then *contentment* describes the ways in which we reflect his attitude. We don't take our cues for peace and satisfaction primarily from our environment, but from Jesus. We aren't trying to copy Jesus mechanically, but we are asking him to work out his character within us. The kind of contentment Paul is urging Timothy (and us) to exhibit is the kind of contentment that develops as a byproduct of intimately knowing Jesus Christ.

DEVOTION

Heavenly Father, whenever we are dissatisfied with what we have, open our eyes to the riches we have in you. Loosen our grip on our material wealth by showing us ways to invest in eternal treasures. Teach us to share what we have and to enjoy the simple pleasures of life.

JOURNALING

In what area of your life do you need God's help to be more content?

FOR FURTHER READING

To complete the books of 1 and 2 Timothy and Titus during this twelve-part study, read 1 Timothy 6:1–21. For more Bible passages on contentment, read Psalm 63:5; Proverbs 19:23; Ecclesiastes 5:10–12; Luke 6:20–23; Philippians 4:10–13; and Hebrews 13:5.

LESSON SEVEN

STRENGTH IN SUFFERING

Join with me in suffering for the gospel, by the power of God. He has saved us and called us to a holy life—not because of anything we have done but because of his own purpose and grace.
2 TIMOTHY 1:8–9

REFLECTION

Are there people who have been sources of encouragement to you during a difficult time in your life? Remember what they did, what they said, and the way they timed their involvement with you. How did they encourage you?

_____

_____

_____

_____

_____

_____

_____

_____

_____

SITUATION

By the time Paul pens his second letter to Timothy, he has gone from the relative freedom he had to move about his congregations in Macedonia to that of a prisoner in a Roman jail. He is virtually alone, with only a few trusted associates around him, and he knows his time on this earth is drawing to a close. With this in mind, Paul pens a deeply personal letter to his partner in ministry, often employing the language one would use with an old and dear friend. Paul has precious final words to pass on to Timothy . . . and also to us. He begins by reviewing his present state of affairs, expressing his thankfulness to God, and encouraging Timothy.

OBSERVATION

Read 2 Timothy 1:1–18 from the New International
Version or the New King James Version.

NEW INTERNATIONAL VERSION

¹ Paul, an apostle of Christ Jesus by the will of God, in keeping with the promise of life that is in Christ Jesus,

² To Timothy, my dear son:

Grace, mercy and peace from God the Father and Christ Jesus our Lord.

³ I thank God, whom I serve, as my ancestors did, with a clear conscience, as night and day I constantly remember you in my prayers. ⁴ Recalling your tears, I long to see you, so that I may be filled with joy. ⁵ I am reminded of your sincere faith, which first lived in your grandmother Lois and in your mother Eunice and, I am persuaded, now lives in you also.

⁶ For this reason I remind you to fan into flame the gift of God, which is in you through the laying on of my hands. ⁷ For the Spirit God gave us does not make us timid, but gives us power, love and self-discipline. ⁸ So do not be ashamed of the testimony about our Lord or of me his prisoner. Rather, join with me in suffering for the gospel, by the power of God. ⁹ He has saved us and called us to a holy life—not because of anything we have done but because of his own purpose and grace. This grace was given us in Christ Jesus before the beginning of time, ¹⁰ but it has now been revealed through the appearing of our Savior, Christ Jesus, who has destroyed death and has brought life and immortality to light through the gospel. ¹¹ And of this gospel I was appointed a herald and an apostle and a teacher. ¹² That is why I am suffering as I am. Yet this is no cause for shame, because I know whom I have believed, and am convinced that he is able to guard what I have entrusted to him until that day.

¹³ What you heard from me, keep as the pattern of sound teaching, with faith and love in Christ Jesus. ¹⁴ Guard the good deposit that was entrusted to you—guard it with the help of the Holy Spirit who lives in us.

¹⁵ You know that everyone in the province of Asia has deserted me, including Phygelus and Hermogenes.

¹⁶ May the Lord show mercy to the household of Onesiphorus, because he often refreshed me and was not ashamed of my chains. ¹⁷ On the contrary, when he was in Rome, he searched hard for me until he found me. ¹⁸ May the Lord grant that he will find mercy from the Lord on that day! You know very well in how many ways he helped me in Ephesus.

NEW KING JAMES VERSION

¹ Paul, an apostle of Jesus Christ by the will of God, according to the promise of life which is in Christ Jesus,

² To Timothy, a beloved son:

Grace, mercy, and peace from God the Father and Christ Jesus our Lord.

³ I thank God, whom I serve with a pure conscience, as my forefathers did, as without ceasing I remember you in my prayers night and day, ⁴ greatly desiring to see you, being mindful of your tears, that I may be filled with joy, ⁵ when I call to remembrance the genuine faith that is in you, which dwelt first in your grandmother Lois and your mother Eunice, and I am persuaded is in you also. ⁶ Therefore I remind you to stir up the gift of God which is in you through the laying on of my hands. ⁷ For God has not given us a spirit of fear, but of power and of love and of a sound mind.

⁸ Therefore do not be ashamed of the testimony of our Lord, nor of me His prisoner, but share with me in the sufferings for the gospel according to the power of God, ⁹ who has saved us and called us with a holy calling, not according to our works, but according to His own purpose and grace which was given to us in Christ Jesus before time began, ¹⁰ but has now been revealed by the appearing of our Savior Jesus Christ, who has abolished death and brought life and immortality to light through the gospel, ¹¹ to which I was appointed a preacher, an apostle, and a teacher of the Gentiles. ¹² For this reason I also suffer these things; nevertheless I am

not ashamed, for I know whom I have believed and am persuaded that He is able to keep what I have committed to Him until that Day.

[13] Hold fast the pattern of sound words which you have heard from me, in faith and love which are in Christ Jesus. [14] That good thing which was committed to you, keep by the Holy Spirit who dwells in us.

[15] This you know, that all those in Asia have turned away from me, among whom are Phygellus and Hermogenes. [16] The Lord grant mercy to the household of Onesiphorus, for he often refreshed me, and was not ashamed of my chain; [17] but when he arrived in Rome, he sought me out very zealously and found me. [18] The Lord grant to him that he may find mercy from the Lord in that Day—and you know very well how many ways he ministered to me at Ephesus.

EXPLORATION

1. How does Paul encourage Timothy to exercise his God-given gifts?

_____

_____

_____

_____

2. What can you learn from Paul's good attitude toward his difficult situation?

_____

_____

3. Why does God allow believers to suffer? How does Paul seem to answer this question?

_____

_____

_____

4. What does Paul say enables Christians to endure trials?

_____

_____

5. In what ways have you seen God protect and provide for his people in the past?

_____

_____

_____

6. What hope does this passage offer to those who are currently suffering?

_____

_____

INSPIRATION

God never creates or parlays evil. "Far be it from God to do evil, from the Almighty to do wrong" (Job 34:10). He is the essence of good. How can he who is good invent anything bad?

And he is sovereign. Scripture repeatedly attributes utter and absolute control to his hand. "The Most High God is sovereign over all kingdoms on earth and sets over them anyone he wishes" (Daniel 5:21). God is good. God is sovereign. Then how are we to factor in the presence of calamities in God's world?

Here is how the Bible does it: God permits it. When the demons begged Jesus to send them into a herd of pigs, he "gave them permission" (Mark 5: 13). Regarding the rebellious, God said, "I defiled them through their gifts . . . that I might fill them with horror so they would know that I am the LORD" (Ezekiel 20:26). The Old Law speaks of the consequence of accidentally killing a person: "However, if it is not done intentionally, but God lets it happen, they are to flee to a place I will designate" (Exodus 21:13).

God at times permits tragedies. He permits the ground to grow dry and stalks to grow bare. He allows Satan to unleash mayhem. But he doesn't allow Satan to triumph. Isn't this the promise of Romans 8:28: "And we know that in all things God works for the good of those who love him, who have been called according to his purpose"? God promises to render beauty out of "all things," not "each thing." The isolated events may be evil, but the ultimate culmination is good.

We see small examples of this in our own lives. When you sip on a cup of coffee and say, "This is good," what are you saying? The plastic bag that contains the beans is good? The beans themselves are good? Hot water is good? A coffee filter is good? No, none of these. Good happens when the ingredients work together: the bag opened, the beans ground into powder, the water heated to the right temperature. It is the collective cooperation of the elements that creates good.

Nothing in the Bible would cause us to call a famine good or a heart attack good or a terrorist attack good. These are terrible calamities, born out of a fallen earth. Yet every message in the Bible compels us to believe that God will mix them with other ingredients and bring good out of them.

But we must let God define *good*. Our definition includes health, comfort, and recognition. His definition? In the case of his Son, Jesus Christ, the good life consisted of struggles, storms, and death. But God worked it all together for the greatest of good: his glory and our salvation. (From *You'll Get Through This* by Max Lucado.)

REACTION

7. What are some ways the Bible shows that God is *always* good and *always* sovereign?

_____

_____

_____

_____

8. How do you explain the presence of calamities and crises in your world?

_____

_____

_____

_____

9. Read 1 Peter 2:21. What difference does it make know that Jesus also dealt with pain and suffering when he was on this earth?

_____

_____

_____

_____

10. Read 1 Peter 5:9. What strength can you draw from knowing "the family of believers throughout the world" is also dealing with trials?

_____

_____

_____

_____

11. In what way does this passage change your attitude toward the problems you face today?

12. What words of encouragement could you offer to a fellow believer who is suffering?

LIFE LESSONS

As Paul illustrates in his opening words in this letter, we can *encourage* (which literally means "inject courage into") others in numerous ways. We can trust them with our personal situation and allow them to care for us. We can remind them of their rich heritage and history and the resources they have to face their circumstances. We can share how Christ motivates us—not because we are so successful, but because of "his own purpose and grace." Today, think about who in your world could benefit deeply from your encouragement.

DEVOTION

Lord, thank you for becoming flesh and blood. Thank you for being willing to face the stress and strain of daily life. It gives us strength and hope to know that you have gone before us and endured without giving up. Help us to remember that you understand our deepest longings, our heartaches, and our dreams.

JOURNALING

When has God helped you through a painful experience in your life? How did he help you?

_____

_____

_____

_____

_____

_____

_____

_____

_____

_____

_____

_____

_____

FOR FURTHER READING

To complete the books of 1 and 2 Timothy and Titus during this twelve-part study, read 2 Timothy 1:1–18. For more Bible passages on suffering, read Job 36:15; Psalm 73:26; Romans 5:3–5; 8:17–18; Philippians 1:29–2:2; 4:13; Hebrews 11:32–40; and 1 Peter 4:12–16.

LESSON EIGHT

PERSEVERING IN CHRIST

For if we died with Him, we shall also live with Him. If we endure, we shall also reign with Him.
2 TIMOTHY 2:11–12 NKJV

REFLECTION

When you think of perseverance, who or what comes to mind? Think of someone you know who has shown courage and determination in a difficult situation. In what way has that person's example influenced you?

SITUATION

Part of Paul's purpose in writing this second letter was to "hand off" to Timothy the ongoing responsibility for spreading the gospel. Timothy would no longer be on temporary assignments—he would now be a journeyman minister. Paul thus encourages Timothy to not only pass on the teachings he has received but also to join with him in suffering "like a good soldier of Christ Jesus" (2:3). He challenges Timothy to keep his focus on what matters most: pleasing God, remaining faithful to his mission, and persevering to the very end.

OBSERVATION

Read 2 Timothy 2:1–13 from the New International Version or the New King James Version.

NEW INTERNATIONAL VERSION

¹ You then, my son, be strong in the grace that is in Christ Jesus. ² And the things you have heard me say in the presence of many witnesses entrust to reliable people who will also be qualified to teach others. ³ Join with me in suffering, like a good soldier of Christ Jesus. ⁴ No one serving as a soldier gets entangled in civilian affairs, but rather tries to please his commanding officer. ⁵ Similarly, anyone who competes as an athlete does not receive the victor's crown except by competing according to the rules. ⁶ The hardworking farmer should be the first to receive a share of the crops. ⁷ Reflect on what I am saying, for the Lord will give you insight into all this.

⁸ Remember Jesus Christ, raised from the dead, descended from David. This is my gospel, ⁹ for which I am suffering even to the point of being chained like a criminal. But God's word is not chained. ¹⁰ Therefore I endure everything for the sake of the elect, that they too may obtain the salvation that is in Christ Jesus, with eternal glory.

¹¹ Here is a trustworthy saying:

If we died with him,
    we will also live with him;
¹² if we endure,
    we will also reign with him.

> If we disown him,
>> he will also disown us;
> ¹³ if we are faithless,
>> he remains faithful,
> for he cannot disown himself.

New King James Version

¹ You therefore, my son, be strong in the grace that is in Christ Jesus.
² And the things that you have heard from me among many witnesses,
commit these to faithful men who will be able to teach others also. ³ You
therefore must endure hardship as a good soldier of Jesus Christ. ⁴ No
one engaged in warfare entangles himself with the affairs of this life, that
he may please him who enlisted him as a soldier. ⁵ And also if anyone
competes in athletics, he is not crowned unless he competes according
to the rules. ⁶ The hardworking farmer must be first to partake of the
crops. ⁷ Consider what I say, and may the Lord give you understanding
in all things.

⁸ Remember that Jesus Christ, of the seed of David, was raised from
the dead according to my gospel, ⁹ for which I suffer trouble as an evil-
doer, even to the point of chains; but the word of God is not chained.
¹⁰ Therefore I endure all things for the sake of the elect, that they also may
obtain the salvation which is in Christ Jesus with eternal glory.

¹¹ This is a faithful saying:

> For if we died with Him,
> We shall also live with Him.
> ¹² If we endure,
> We shall also reign with Him.
> If we deny Him,
> He also will deny us.
> ¹³ If we are faithless,
> He remains faithful;
> He cannot deny Himself.

EXPLORATION

1. What responsibility do believers have to teach others what they have learned?

2. In what way does being a Christian compare to being a soldier, an athlete, or a farmer?

3. As a "good soldier of Christ Jesus," why is it critical to seek to please your "commanding officer" above all others (verse 4)?

4. What does this passage say about patiently enduring the troubles you encounter in life?

5. In what way will God reward those who accept suffering for his sake?

6. What hope does the Bible offer to those who are struggling to remain faithful to God?

INSPIRATION

Since God is more moved by our hurt than our eloquence, he responds. That's what fathers do.

That's exactly what Jim Redmond did.

His son Derek, a twenty-six-year-old Briton, was favored to win the four-hundred-meter race in the 1992 Barcelona Olympics. Halfway into his semifinal heat, a fiery pain seared through his right leg. He crumpled to the track with a torn hamstring.

As the medical attendants were approaching, Redmond fought to his feet. "It was animal instinct," he would later say. He set out hopping, pushing away the coaches in a crazed attempt to finish the race.

When he reached the stretch, a big man pushed through the crowd. He was wearing a T-shirt that read "Have you hugged your child today?" and a hat that challenged, "Just Do It." The man was Jim Redmond, Derek's father.

"You don't have to do this," he told his weeping son.

"Yes, I do," Derek declared.

"Well, then," said Jim, "we're going to finish this together."

And they did. Jim wrapped Derek's arm around his shoulder and helped him hobble to the finish line. Fighting off security men, the son's head sometimes buried in the father's shoulder, they stayed in Derek's lane to the end.

The crowd clapped, then stood, then cheered, and then wept as the father and the son finished the race.

What made the father do it? What made the father leave the stands to meet his son on the track? Was it the strength of his child? No, it was the pain of his child. His son was hurt and fighting to complete the race. So the father came to help him finish.

God does the same. Our prayers may be awkward. Our attempts may be feeble. But since the power of prayer is in the one who hears it and not the one who says them, our prayers do make a difference. (From *He Still Moves Stones* by Max Lucado.)

REACTION

7. How have you seen your heavenly Father respond when you were in a time of suffering?

_____

_____

_____

_____

8. How has your faith in God's goodness and mercy helped you persevere through a time of disappointment or discouragement?

9. Read 1 Peter 1:6–9. What is the problem with trying to avoid trials in your life?

_____

_____

10. How can prayer make a difference in the way you view your problems?

11. In what ways does your eternal hope in Christ help you to persevere?

12. In what ways would you live differently if you did *not* believe in eternal life?

LIFE LESSONS

Perseverance can be described as faith stretched out over time. However, perseverance must also be *lived* out one day at a time, for as Jesus pointed out "each day has enough trouble of its own" (Matthew 6:34). The athlete, soldier, and farmer that Paul uses to illustrate perseverance must all wait to see the results of their efforts. Immediate feedback and benefits are nice, but the most important aspects of life require waiting—and waiting requires faith and character.

DEVOTION

Father, when trials come, doubts tend to creep into our minds. We wonder whether we will feel your presence and experience your power. But you have promised to be with us always. So we ask you to help us depend on you to carry us through the tough times. Remind us that one day we will live with you and give us the strength to persevere until that day.

JOURNALING

In what area of your life are you tempted to give up hope? How can you persevere in this area?

FOR FURTHER READING

To complete the books of 1 and 2 Timothy and Titus during this twelve-part study, read 2 Timothy 2:1–13. For more Bible passages on perseverance, read Romans 5:3–4; 1 Timothy 4:15–16; Hebrews 10:35–39; 12:1–3; James 1:2–4; 5:11; and Revelation 2:2–3.

LESSON NINE

WORKERS PLEASING TO GOD

Do your best to present yourself to God as one approved, a worker who does not need to be ashamed and who correctly handles the word of truth.
2 TIMOTHY 2:15

REFLECTION

Think about your personal measurement of success. What questions do you use to decide if an effort in which you have been involved is worthwhile or successful? Consider how God measures success. Why and how do you think God chooses people for his work?

_____

_____

_____

_____

SITUATION

Paul was well aware of the continual dangers of false teachers and trouble-makers in the church. Given this, even in this deeply personal letter, Paul feels compelled to remind Timothy to watch out for foolish talk and evil teaching. He urges Timothy to be a leader by the example of his life as well as the instruction he gives to others. Paul continues to offer his notes for how a servant of the Lord should act as well as his personal insights about pursuing the spiritual life.

OBSERVATION

Read 2 Timothy 2:14–26 from the New International Version or the New King James Version.

NEW INTERNATIONAL VERSION

¹⁴ Keep reminding God's people of these things. Warn them before God against quarreling about words; it is of no value, and only ruins those who listen. ¹⁵ Do your best to present yourself to God as one approved, a worker who does not need to be ashamed and who correctly handles

the word of truth. [16] Avoid godless chatter, because those who indulge in it will become more and more ungodly. [17] Their teaching will spread like gangrene. Among them are Hymenaeus and Philetus, [18] who have departed from the truth. They say that the resurrection has already taken place, and they destroy the faith of some. [19] Nevertheless, God's solid foundation stands firm, sealed with this inscription: "The Lord knows those who are his," and, "Everyone who confesses the name of the Lord must turn away from wickedness."

[20] In a large house there are articles not only of gold and silver, but also of wood and clay; some are for special purposes and some for common use. [21] Those who cleanse themselves from the latter will be instruments for special purposes, made holy, useful to the Master and prepared to do any good work.

[22] Flee the evil desires of youth and pursue righteousness, faith, love and peace, along with those who call on the Lord out of a pure heart. [23] Don't have anything to do with foolish and stupid arguments, because you know they produce quarrels. [24] And the Lord's servant must not be quarrelsome but must be kind to everyone, able to teach, not resentful. [25] Opponents must be gently instructed, in the hope that God will grant them repentance leading them to a knowledge of the truth, [26] and that they will come to their senses and escape from the trap of the devil, who has taken them captive to do his will.

New King James Version

[14] Remind them of these things, charging them before the Lord not to strive about words to no profit, to the ruin of the hearers. [15] Be diligent to present yourself approved to God, a worker who does not need to be ashamed, rightly dividing the word of truth. [16] But shun profane and idle babblings, for they will increase to more ungodliness. [17] And their message will spread like cancer. Hymenaeus and Philetus are of this sort, [18] who have strayed concerning the truth, saying that the resurrection is already past; and they overthrow the faith of some. [19] Nevertheless the solid foundation of God stands, having this seal: "The Lord knows those

who are His," and, "Let everyone who names the name of Christ depart from iniquity."

²⁰ But in a great house there are not only vessels of gold and silver, but also of wood and clay, some for honor and some for dishonor. ²¹ Therefore if anyone cleanses himself from the latter, he will be a vessel for honor, sanctified and useful for the Master, prepared for every good work. ²² Flee also youthful lusts; but pursue righteousness, faith, love, peace with those who call on the Lord out of a pure heart. ²³ But avoid foolish and ignorant disputes, knowing that they generate strife. ²⁴ And a servant of the Lord must not quarrel but be gentle to all, able to teach, patient, ²⁵ in humility correcting those who are in opposition, if God perhaps will grant them repentance, so that they may know the truth, ²⁶ and that they may come to their senses and escape the snare of the devil, having been taken captive by him to do his will.

EXPLORATION

1. What are some of the characteristics of a worker who is pleasing to God?

_____

_____

_____

2. Why should believers avoid "godless chatter" or "idle babblings" (verse 16)?

_____

_____

_____

3. What is the problem with engaging in "foolish and stupid arguments" (verse 23)?

_____

_____

_____

4. Why is consistent study of God's Word essential to the Christian life?

5. What kind of person does God use to fulfill his special purposes?

6. In what ways can believers help those who are confused about the truth?

INSPIRATION

In the shop of a blacksmith, there are three types of tools.

There are tools on the junkpile: outdated, broken, dull, rusty. They sit in the cobwebbed corner, useless to their master, oblivious to their calling.

There are tools on the anvil: melted down, molten hot, moldable, changeable. They lie on the anvil, being shaped by their master, accepting their calling.

There are tools of usefulness: sharpened, primed, defined, mobile. They lie ready in the blacksmith's tool chest, available to their master, fulfilling their calling.

Some people lie useless: lives broken, talents wasting, fires quenched, dreams dashed. They are tossed in with the scrap iron, in desperate need of repair, with no notion of purpose.

Others lie on the anvil: hearts open, hungry to change, wounds healing, vision clearing. They welcome the painful pounding of the blacksmith's hammer, longing to be rebuilt, begging to be called.

Others lie in their Master's hands: well-tuned, noncompromising, polished, productive. They respond to their Master's forearm, demanding nothing, surrendering all.

We are all somewhere in the blacksmith's shop. We are either on the scrap pile, on the anvil, in the Master's hands, or in the tool chest. (Some of us have been in all three.) From the shelves to the workbench, from the water to the fire . . . I'm sure that somewhere you'll see yourself . . . The rubbish pile of broken tools, the anvil of recasting, the hands of the Master—it's a simultaneously joyful and painful voyage.

And for you who make the journey—who leave the heap and enter the fire, dare to be pounded on God's anvil, and doggedly seek to discover your own purpose—take courage, for you await the privilege of being called "God's chosen instruments." (From *Shaped by God* by Max Lucado.)

REACTION

7. Where would you say you are right now in the "blacksmith's shop"? Why?

_____

_____

_____

_____

8. How does God prepare you to serve him? What kinds of "tools" does he use to make you an effective instrument for him?

_____

_____

_____

9. What are some of the challenges and rewards of being a servant of God?

10. What gifts do you feel God has given you to serve his purposes?

11. How can you determine whether your work pleases God? What is God looking for in you?

12. What spiritual disciplines can keep you more focused on doing what God wants you to do?

LIFE LESSONS

Paul says one of our goals as Christians is to have a "pure heart" (2 Timothy 2:22). He expands that concept by helping us see we must *find* our place in the body of Christ and *fill* our place in the body of Christ. Even while we are learning what it means to serve, we can serve. We can take the expectations of others into account, but ultimately we want to fulfill God's purposes and receive his approval. A persistent desire to accomplish this flows from a pure heart.

DEVOTION

Father, thank you for working through us to accomplish great things for your kingdom. We appreciate the privilege of being called your people and being used by you. Transform us into the kind of people suitable for your work and use us for your special purposes.

JOURNALING

What is a task you are doing that is pleasing to God? How have you seen God help you fulfill it?

FOR FURTHER READING

To complete the books of 1 and 2 Timothy and Titus during this twelve-part study, read 2 Timothy 2:14–26. For more Bible passages on becoming a worker pleasing to God, read John 6:27; 1 Corinthians 3:5–9; 2 Corinthians 5:9–10; Colossians 3:23; 1 Thessalonians 4:11–12; 5:12–13; 2 Thessalonians 3:6–13; and Hebrews 6:10–12.

LESSON TEN

FOLLOWING THE TRUTH

*Continue in the things which you have
learned . . . and that from childhood you have
known the Holy Scriptures, which are able to
make you wise for salvation through faith.*
2 TIMOTHY 3:14–15 NKJV

REFLECTION

Think about one or two of the values your parents tried to teach you when you were growing up. In what ways have those truths helped you throughout your life?

_____

_____

_____

_____

SITUATION

Paul concludes his personal letter to Timothy by reminding him that while there will always be troublemakers in this fallen world—just as there was in the time of Moses—in the end their "folly will be clear to everyone" (3:9). Paul's urging to Timothy is to have nothing to do with such people, but to continually strive to lead a godly life by following the teachings he had learned. In the same way, Paul's challenge to us is to continually seek to live a life pleasing to God by following the teaching we receive in his inspired Word—the Bible.

OBSERVATION

Read 2 Timothy 3:1–17 from the New International Version or the New King James Version.

New International Version

¹ But mark this: There will be terrible times in the last days. ² People will be lovers of themselves, lovers of money, boastful, proud, abusive, disobedient to their parents, ungrateful, unholy, ³ without love, unforgiving, slanderous, without self-control, brutal, not lovers of the good,

⁴ treacherous, rash, conceited, lovers of pleasure rather than lovers of God— ⁵ having a form of godliness but denying its power. Have nothing to do with such people.

⁶ They are the kind who worm their way into homes and gain control over gullible women, who are loaded down with sins and are swayed by all kinds of evil desires, ⁷ always learning but never able to come to a knowledge of the truth. ⁸ Just as Jannes and Jambres opposed Moses, so also these teachers oppose the truth. They are men of depraved minds, who, as far as the faith is concerned, are rejected. ⁹ But they will not get very far because, as in the case of those men, their folly will be clear to everyone.

¹⁰ You, however, know all about my teaching, my way of life, my purpose, faith, patience, love, endurance, ¹¹ persecutions, sufferings—what kinds of things happened to me in Antioch, Iconium and Lystra, the persecutions I endured. Yet the Lord rescued me from all of them. ¹² In fact, everyone who wants to live a godly life in Christ Jesus will be persecuted, ¹³ while evildoers and impostors will go from bad to worse, deceiving and being deceived. ¹⁴ But as for you, continue in what you have learned and have become convinced of, because you know those from whom you learned it, ¹⁵ and how from infancy you have known the Holy Scriptures, which are able to make you wise for salvation through faith in Christ Jesus. ¹⁶ All Scripture is God-breathed and is useful for teaching, rebuking, correcting and training in righteousness, ¹⁷ so that the servant of God may be thoroughly equipped for every good work.

NEW KING JAMES VERSION

¹ But know this, that in the last days perilous times will come: ² For men will be lovers of themselves, lovers of money, boasters, proud, blasphemers, disobedient to parents, unthankful, unholy, ³ unloving, unforgiving, slanderers, without self-control, brutal, despisers of good, ⁴ traitors, headstrong, haughty, lovers of pleasure rather than lovers of God, ⁵ having a form of godliness but denying its power. And from such people turn away! ⁶ For of this sort are those who creep into households and make captives of

gullible women loaded down with sins, led away by various lusts, [7] always learning and never able to come to the knowledge of the truth. [8] Now as Jannes and Jambres resisted Moses, so do these also resist the truth: men of corrupt minds, disapproved concerning the faith; [9] but they will progress no further, for their folly will be manifest to all, as theirs also was.

[10] But you have carefully followed my doctrine, manner of life, purpose, faith, longsuffering, love, perseverance, [11] persecutions, afflictions, which happened to me at Antioch, at Iconium, at Lystra—what persecutions I endured. And out of them all the Lord delivered me. [12] Yes, and all who desire to live godly in Christ Jesus will suffer persecution. [13] But evil men and impostors will grow worse and worse, deceiving and being deceived. [14] But you must continue in the things which you have learned and been assured of, knowing from whom you have learned them, [15] and that from childhood you have known the Holy Scriptures, which are able to make you wise for salvation through faith which is in Christ Jesus.

[16] All Scripture is given by inspiration of God, and is profitable for doctrine, for reproof, for correction, for instruction in righteousness, [17] that the man of God may be complete, thoroughly equipped for every good work.

EXPLORATION

1. What does Paul say will occur during "the last days" (verse 1)?

2. What does Paul say is the danger of those who are "lovers of themselves" and "[have] a form of godliness but [deny] its power" when it comes to believers in the church (verses 2, 5)?

3. How should believers be different from those who are not following Christ?

4. How can believers protect themselves from worldly pressures?

5. What does Paul say will eventually happen to those who oppose the work of the gospel?

6. How does studying the Bible equip you to do God's work? What is involved in this beyond just having a copy of the Bible on your shelf or on your smartphone?

INSPIRATION

The apostle Paul warned that many will follow the false teachers, not knowing that in feeding upon what these people say they are taking the devil's poison into their own lives. Thousands of people in every walk of life are being deceived today. False teachers use high-sounding words that seem like the height of logic, scholarship, and sophistication. They are intellectually clever and crafty in their sophistry. They are adept at beguiling men and women whose spiritual foundations are weak.

These false teachers have departed from the faith of God revealed in the Scripture. . . . The apostle Paul warned, "Now the Spirit expressly says that in latter times some will depart from the faith, giving heed to deceiving spirits and doctrines of demons, speaking lies in hypocrisy, having their own conscience seared with a hot iron" (1 Timothy 4:1–2 NKJV).

Paul later wrote to Timothy, "For the time will come when they will not endure sound doctrine, but according to their own desires, because they have itching ears, they will heap up for themselves teachers; and they will turn their ears away from the truth, and be turned aside to fables" (2 Timothy 4:3–4 NKJV). Doesn't this sound familiar today?

God's plan is not abstract or unclear. It is not a secret. He says very clearly, "I love you!" He has called tens of thousands all over the world to proclaim His love to the world and to call every man, woman, and child to His loving arms. I can think of no better example than the thousands of "barefoot preachers" and other itinerant evangelists we helped train. . . .

Today that mighty army of traveling preachers from every corner of the world is traveling from village to village and house to house preaching the good news of God's love. Why do they do it? For the money? No, they receive almost no support for what they do. . . . Do they do it for fame and fortune? There is none. In most cases only God knows what good works these humble, sincere pastors have done.

They do it because Jesus Christ is alive! He is living in their hearts, and that good news is something worthy to share with the world. They are compelled by the life that is in them to tell everyone that Jesus is Lord. If Jesus Christ is not the Son of God, nothing matters. But if he is, nothing else matters! (From *Storm Warning* by Billy Graham.)

REACTION

7. In what ways does our society try to beguile those "whose spiritual foundations are weak"?

_____

_____

_____

_____

8. How does bending or distorting God's truth only serve to hurt people?

_____

_____

_____

_____

9. What are some reasons why people often choose to reject or oppose the truth?

_____

_____

_____

_____

10. What motivates you to trust in and follow the teachings in God's Word?

_____

_____

_____

11. How can you guard the truth of the gospel when interacting with others?

_____

_____

_____

_____

12. What are some specific ways you can show respect for God's Word this week?

_____

_____

_____

_____

LIFE LESSONS

The practical side of Paul's words in this passage are clear: our lives must be guided by God's Word. Paul reminded Timothy (and us) that there are various "profitable" ways to apply Scripture. Every passage we read offers us one or more of the following gifts: truth (doctrine), conviction (reproof), direction (correction), and training (instruction in righteousness). But merely _knowing_ that God's Word has been given to accomplish these purposes in us is not enough. We must actually submit our lives to God's Word by _obeying_ it.

DEVOTION

Father, thank you for giving us your Word and for teaching us what is good and true. Keep us from deceptive teaching and twisted versions of the truth. Help us to guard our lives with the truth—for your Word is life.

JOURNALING

In what ways do you need to *follow* and *obey* God's Word more closely in your life?

_____

_____

_____

_____

_____

_____

_____

_____

_____

_____

_____

_____

_____

_____

_____

_____

_____

_____

_____

_____

_____

_____

_____

_____

_____

FOR FURTHER READING

To complete the books of 1 and 2 Timothy and Titus during this twelve-part study, read 2 Timothy 3:1–4:22. For more Bible passages on guarding the truth, read Psalm 119:30; Proverbs 7:1–4; Acts 20:28–32; 1 Corinthians 16:13; 1 Timothy 6:20–21; 3 John 1: 3–4; Jude 1:3; and Revelation 22:18–19.

LESSON ELEVEN

ROLE MODELS

In your teaching show integrity, seriousness and soundness of speech that cannot be condemned, so that those who oppose you may be ashamed because they have nothing bad to say about us.

TITUS 2:7–8

REFLECTION

Who do you consider to be your role models? In what ways have they influenced you for good?

SITUATION

Although there was less history between Paul and Titus, the apostle trusted his co-worker with the important assignment of ministering in Crete. Titus had the responsibility for shaping the church of Christ that was developing throughout the towns on the island. In many ways his instruction parallels his words in 1 Timothy, in that he lists qualifications for church leaders (see 1:5–16) and then instructs on how to guide specific groups of people within the church. He encourages Titus to "rebuke will all authority" and not let anyone despise him (see 2:15).

OBSERVATION

*Read Titus 2:1–15 from the New International
Version or the New King James Version.*

NEW INTERNATIONAL VERSION

[1] You, however, must teach what is appropriate to sound doctrine. [2] Teach the older men to be temperate, worthy of respect, self-controlled, and sound in faith, in love and in endurance.

[3] Likewise, teach the older women to be reverent in the way they live, not to be slanderers or addicted to much wine, but to teach what is good. [4] Then they can urge the younger women to love their husbands and children, [5] to be self-controlled and pure, to be busy at home, to be kind, and to be subject to their husbands, so that no one will malign the word of God.

[6] Similarly, encourage the young men to be self-controlled. [7] In everything set them an example by doing what is good. In your teaching show integrity, seriousness [8] and soundness of speech that cannot be condemned, so that those who oppose you may be ashamed because they have nothing bad to say about us.

[9] Teach slaves to be subject to their masters in everything, to try to please them, not to talk back to them, [10] and not to steal from them, but to show that they can be fully trusted, so that in every way they will make the teaching about God our Savior attractive.

[11] For the grace of God has appeared that offers salvation to all people. [12] It teaches us to say "No" to ungodliness and worldly passions, and to live self-controlled, upright and godly lives in this present age, [13] while we wait for the blessed hope—the appearing of the glory of our great God and Savior, Jesus Christ, [14] who gave himself for us to redeem us from all wickedness and to purify for himself a people that are his very own, eager to do what is good.

[15] These, then, are the things you should teach. Encourage and rebuke with all authority. Do not let anyone despise you.

NEW KING JAMES VERSION

¹ But as for you, speak the things which are proper for sound doctrine: ² that the older men be sober, reverent, temperate, sound in faith, in love, in patience; ³ the older women likewise, that they be reverent in behavior, not slanderers, not given to much wine, teachers of good things— ⁴ that they admonish the young women to love their husbands, to love their children, ⁵ to be discreet, chaste, homemakers, good, obedient to their own husbands, that the word of God may not be blasphemed.

⁶ Likewise, exhort the young men to be sober-minded, ⁷ in all things showing yourself to be a pattern of good works; in doctrine showing integrity, reverence, incorruptibility, ⁸ sound speech that cannot be condemned, that one who is an opponent may be ashamed, having nothing evil to say of you.

⁹ Exhort bondservants to be obedient to their own masters, to be well pleasing in all things, not answering back, ¹⁰ not pilfering, but showing all good fidelity, that they may adorn the doctrine of God our Savior in all things.

¹¹ For the grace of God that brings salvation has appeared to all men, ¹² teaching us that, denying ungodliness and worldly lusts, we should live soberly, righteously, and godly in the present age, ¹³ looking for the blessed hope and glorious appearing of our great God and Savior Jesus Christ, ¹⁴ who gave Himself for us, that He might redeem us from every lawless deed and purify for Himself His own special people, zealous for good works.

¹⁵ Speak these things, exhort, and rebuke with all authority. Let no one despise you.

EXPLORATION

1. What attitudes and behaviors should older men and women exemplify for the younger generations?

_____

_____

_____

2. Why is it more effective to *show* people how to live rather than just *tell* them?

_____

_____

_____

_____

_____

3. In what ways can you attract others to the teaching of God?

_____

_____

_____

_____

4. How can you earn the right to give advice to others about how to live for God?

_____

_____

_____

_____

_____

5. Why is it important to live in continual expectation of the "appearing of the glory of our great God and Savior" (verse 13)?

_____

_____

_____

_____

6. Why do Christian leaders deserve respect? In what ways can you express respect to them?

_____

_____

_____

_____

_____

INSPIRATION

Now I see why powerful people often wear sunglasses—the spotlight blinds them to reality. They suffer from a delusion that power means something (it doesn't). They suffer from the misconception that titles make a difference (they don't). They are under the impression that earthly authority will make a heavenly difference (it won't).

Can I prove my point? Take this quiz. Name the ten wealthiest men in the world. Name the last ten Heisman trophy winners. Name the last ten winners of the Miss America contest. Name eight people who have won the Nobel or Pulitzer prize. How about the last ten Academy Award winners for best picture or the last decade's worth of World Series winners?

How did you do? I didn't do well either. With the exception of you trivia hounds, none of us remember the headliners of yesterday too well. Surprising how quickly we forget, isn't it? And what I've mentioned above are no second-rate achievements. These are the best in their fields. But the applause dies. Awards tarnish. Achievements are forgotten. Accolades and certificates are buried with their owners.

Here's another quiz. See how you do on this one. Think of three people you enjoy spending time with. Name ten people who have taught you something worthwhile. Name five friends who have helped you in a difficult time. List a few teachers who have aided your journey through school. Name half-a-dozen heroes whose stories have inspired you.

Easier? It was for me, too. The lesson? The people who make a difference are not the ones with the credentials, but the ones with the concern. (From *And the Angels Were Silent* by Max Lucado.)

REACTION

7. Why is it so easy to quickly forget the achievements and accomplishments of others?

_____

_____

_____

_____

_____

8. Why is so much harder to forget the example of those who have been role models?

_____

_____

_____

_____

_____

9. What happens when believers reach out to help others in the family of God?

_____

_____

_____

_____

10. What personally motivates you to live for God?

_____

_____

_____

_____

11. Who in your life can help keep you accountable in your Christian walk? What do you think that accountability needs to involve?

12. Who is someone you can encourage in the faith? How will you do it?

LIFE LESSONS

People with clear purpose can navigate the rough terrain of life. Those who walk through a wilderness can keep their path straight if they have a distant reference point: "looking for the blessed hope and glorious appearing of our great God and Savior Jesus Christ" (Titus 2:13 NKJV). Christ is the only reference point that can be seen from any place in our lives—and he will surely guide us home. As Paul reminds us, we're not walking through the wilderness alone. We journey with lots of company: younger believers, older believers, and those in different seasons of life and different spheres of influence. How we choose to get along as we make our way indicates how carefully we are keeping our eyes on Jesus, our ultimate hope.

DEVOTION

Father, thank you for the role models you have given us. Remind us that our actions and attitudes make a difference in the lives of others, either for good or for bad. We pray that you would empower us through your Holy Spirit to set a positive example for others to follow.

JOURNALING

What do your daily actions and attitudes reveal to others about your beliefs?

_____

_____

_____

_____

_____

_____

_____

_____

_____

_____

_____

_____

_____

_____

_____

_____

_____

_____

_____

_____

_____

_____

_____

_____

_____

_____

_____

_____

_____

FOR FURTHER READING

To complete the books of 1 and 2 Timothy and Titus during this twelve-part study, read Titus 1:1–2:15. For more Bible passages on setting a good example, read 2 Thessalonians 3:9; 1 Timothy 4:12; Hebrews 12:3; James 5:10; and 1 Peter 2:21.

LESSON TWELVE

LIFE IN THE SPIRIT

*Not by works of righteousness which we have
done, but according to His mercy He saved
us, through the washing of regeneration
and renewing of the Holy Spirit.*

Titus 3:5 NKJV

REFLECTION

Think of one person who lives what you would consider a "Spirit-filled life" and how that person approaches obstacles and difficulties. Also think about Note how he or she relates to other people. What evidences of God's power do you notice in that person's life?

SITUATION

In contrast to his fatherly style with Timothy, Paul communicates to Titus in a brief and almost memo-like style. He makes little mention of the feelings or struggles that Titus is experiencing, and he issues his directives with almost a tone of expectation. Perhaps the reason for this is because Paul, being a student of humanity, recognized this was the most effective way to encourage his co-worker . . . or perhaps Titus was older and had already proven his abilities. Regardless, Paul's trust in his associate is clear as he closes his letter, reminding Titus to continue leading the believers to do good, and requesting his presence as soon as possible.

OBSERVATION

Read Titus 3:1–15 from the New International Version or the New King James Version.

New International Version
[1] Remind the people to be subject to rulers and authorities, to be obedient, to be ready to do whatever is good, [2] to slander no one, to be peaceable and considerate, and always to be gentle toward everyone.

[3] At one time we too were foolish, disobedient, deceived and enslaved by all kinds of passions and pleasures. We lived in malice and envy, being hated and hating one another. [4] But when the kindness and love of God our Savior appeared, [5] he saved us, not because of righteous things we had done, but because of his mercy. He saved us through the washing of rebirth and renewal by the Holy Spirit, [6] whom he poured out on us generously through Jesus Christ our Savior, [7] so that, having been justified by his grace, we might become heirs having the hope of eternal life. [8] This is a trustworthy saying. And I want you to stress these things, so that those who have trusted in God may be careful to devote themselves to doing what is good. These things are excellent and profitable for everyone.

[9] But avoid foolish controversies and genealogies and arguments and quarrels about the law, because these are unprofitable and useless. [10] Warn a divisive person once, and then warn them a second time. After that, have nothing to do with them. [11] You may be sure that such people are warped and sinful; they are self-condemned.

[12] As soon as I send Artemas or Tychicus to you, do your best to come to me at Nicopolis, because I have decided to winter there. [13] Do everything you can to help Zenas the lawyer and Apollos on their way and see that they have everything they need. [14] Our people must learn to devote themselves to doing what is good, in order to provide for urgent needs and not live unproductive lives.

[15] Everyone with me sends you greetings. Greet those who love us in the faith.

Grace be with you all.

NEW KING JAMES VERSION

[1] Remind them to be subject to rulers and authorities, to obey, to be ready for every good work, [2] to speak evil of no one, to be peaceable, gentle, showing all humility to all men. [3] For we ourselves were also once foolish, disobedient, deceived, serving various lusts and pleasures, living in malice and envy, hateful and hating one another. [4] But when the kindness and the love of God our Savior toward man appeared, [5] not by works of

righteousness which we have done, but according to His mercy He saved us, through the washing of regeneration and renewing of the Holy Spirit, ⁶ whom He poured out on us abundantly through Jesus Christ our Savior, ⁷ that having been justified by His grace we should become heirs according to the hope of eternal life.

⁸ This is a faithful saying, and these things I want you to affirm constantly, that those who have believed in God should be careful to maintain good works. These things are good and profitable to men.

⁹ But avoid foolish disputes, genealogies, contentions, and strivings about the law; for they are unprofitable and useless. ¹⁰ Reject a divisive man after the first and second admonition, ¹¹ knowing that such a person is warped and sinning, being self-condemned.

¹² When I send Artemas to you, or Tychicus, be diligent to come to me at Nicopolis, for I have decided to spend the winter there. ¹³ Send Zenas the lawyer and Apollos on their journey with haste, that they may lack nothing. ¹⁴ And let our people also learn to maintain good works, to meet urgent needs, that they may not be unfruitful.

¹⁵ All who are with me greet you. Greet those who love us in the faith. Grace be with you all. Amen.

EXPLORATION

1. What do you think Paul states that you are to be subject to rulers and authorities?

_____

_____

2. What are some of the ways your life should change after you accept Christ?

_____

3. In what ways does sin enslave people?

4. Why are good deeds unable to make a person right with God?

5. What does Christ's saving work do for those who accept him?

6. How does the Holy Spirit make someone a "new person"?

INSPIRATION

Can a scientist study stars and never weep at their splendor? Dissect a rose and never notice its perfume? Can a theologian study the Law until he decodes the shoe size of Moses but still lack the peace needed for a good night's sleep?

Maybe that's why Nicodemus comes at night. He is tired and can't sleep. Tired of rules and regulations but no rest. Nicodemus is looking for a change. And he has a hunch Jesus can give it. Though Nicodemus asks no question, Jesus offers him an answer. "Very truly I tell you, no one can see the kingdom of God unless they are born again" (John 3:3).

This is radical language. To see the kingdom of God you need an unprecedented rebirth from God. Nicodemus staggers at the elephantine thought. "How can someone be born when they are old? . . . Surely they cannot enter a second time into their mother's womb to be born!" (verse 4). . . .

Nicodemus seems to be saying, "Jesus, I've got the spiritual energy of an old mule. How do you expect me to be born again when I can't even remember if figs can be eaten on the Sabbath? I'm an old man. How can a man be born when he is old?" According to Christ, the new birth must come from a new place. "The truth is, no one can enter the Kingdom of God without being born of water and the Spirit. Humans can reproduce only human life, but the Holy Spirit gives new life from heaven" (verses 5–6 NLT).

Could Jesus be more direct? "*No one* can enter the Kingdom of God without being born of water and the Spirit." You want to go to heaven? Doesn't matter how religious you are or how many rules you keep. You need a new birth. You need to be "born of water and the Spirit."

God gives no sponge baths. He washes us from head to toe. Paul reflected on his conversion and wrote: "He washed away our sins, giving us a new birth and new life through the Holy Spirit" (Titus 3:5 NLT) . . .

When you believe in Christ, Christ works a miracle in you. "When you believed in Christ, he identified you as his own by giving you the Holy Spirit" (Ephesians 1:13 NLT). You are permanently purified and empowered by God himself. The message of Jesus to the religious person is simple: *It's not what you do. It's what I do. I have moved in.*

And in time you can say with Paul, "I myself no longer live, but Christ lives in me" (Galatians 2:20 NLT). (From *Next Door Savior* by Max Lucado.)

REACTION

7. What is the role of the Holy Spirit in renewing and equipping believers (see also Luke 10:21, John 14:26, Acts 4:31, and 2 Peter 1:21)?

_____

_____

_____

8. What does it mean to be led by the Spirit? How is the presence of the Holy Spirit like an internal GPS guidance system?

_____

_____

_____

9. What role does the Holy Spirit play in _your_ life?

_____

_____

10. Why is it important to remember you are saved by God's grace— and not by anything that you have done?

_____

_____

_____

11. If you are saved by faith and not works, why should you still work to live a righteous life?

_____

_____

_____

12. What happens when you try to do what is right in your own strength instead of depending on the Holy Spirit? Describe a personal experience that illustrates the point for you.

_____

_____

_____

LIFE LESSONS

Unless you've memorized 1 and 2 Timothy and Titus, you've discovered there are simply too many practical guidelines in these brief letters to remember them all. Depending on your place in life, you may want to review the letters often and list the guidelines that particularly apply to your relationships and duties. In his closing to Titus, Paul highlights the particular role of each person in the Trinity in your salvation—God the Father, Jesus Christ your Savior, and the Holy Spirit your Renewer. Everything you do and have flows out of what God has already done.

DEVOTION

Lord, it is through your grace alone that we stand before you. We need your help even to live for you. Fill us with wisdom, renew our hearts and minds, and attune our ears to your Spirit's voice. Let our lives be testimonies of the Holy Spirit's power.

JOURNALING

How will you thank God today for the changes the Holy Spirit has made in your life?

FOR FURTHER READING

To complete the books of 1 and 2 Timothy and Titus during this twelve-part study, read Titus 3:1–15. For more Bible passages on living in the Spirit, read John 14:15–17; Acts 1:8; 2:17–18; Romans 8:5–17; 1 Corinthians 3:16; 12:13; Galatians 5:25; and 2 Peter 1:21.

LEADER'S GUIDE FOR SMALL GROUPS

Thank you for your willingness to lead a group through *Life Lessons from 1 and 2 Timothy and Titus*. The rewards of being a leader are different from those of participating, and we hope you find your own walk with Jesus deepened by this experience. During the twelve lessons in this study, you will guide your group through selected passages in 1 Timothy, 2 Timothy, and Titus and explore the key themes of the letters. There are several elements in this leader's guide that will help you as you structure your study and reflection time, so be sure to follow along and take advantage of each one.

BEFORE YOU BEGIN

Before your first meeting, make sure the group members have their own copy of the *Life Lessons from 1 and 2 Timothy and Titus* study guide so they can follow along and have their answers written out ahead of time. Alternately, you can hand out the guides at your first meeting and give the group some time to look over the material and ask any preliminary questions. Be sure to send a sheet around the room during that first meeting and have the members write down their name, phone number, and email address so you can keep in touch with them during the week.

There are several ways to structure the duration of the study. You can choose to cover each lesson individually for a total of twelve weeks of discussion, or you can combine two lessons together per week for a total of six weeks of discussion. You can also choose to have the group members read just the selected passages of Scripture given in each lesson, or they can cover the entire books of 1 Timothy, 2 Timothy, and Titus by reading the material listed in the "For Further Reading" section at the end of each lesson. The following table illustrates these options:

Twelve-Week Format

Week	Lessons Covered	Simplified Reading	Expanded Reading
1	Christ's Power to Save	1 Timothy 1:12–20	1 Timothy 1:1–20
2	Prayer and Worship	1 Timothy 2:1–15	1 Timothy 2:1–15
3	Leading Others	1 Timothy 3:1–16	1 Timothy 3:1–16
4	Believing the Truth	1 Timothy 4:1–16	1 Timothy 4:1–16
5	Managing Relationships	1 Timothy 5:1–21	1 Timothy 5:1–25
6	Finding Contentment	1 Timothy 6:6–19	1 Timothy 6:1–21
7	Strength in Suffering	2 Timothy 1:1–18	2 Timothy 1:1–18
8	Persevering in Christ	2 Timothy 2:1–13	2 Timothy 2:1–13
9	Workers Pleasing to God	2 Timothy 2:14–26	2 Timothy 2:14–26
10	Following the Truth	2 Timothy 3:1–17	2 Timothy 3:1–4:22
11	Role Models	Titus 2:1–15	Titus 1:1–2:15
12	Life in the Spirit	Titus 3:1–15	Titus 3:1–15

Six-Week Format

Week	Lessons Covered	Simplified Reading	Expanded Reading
1	Christ's Power to Save / Prayer and Worship	1 Timothy 1:12–2:15	1 Timothy 1:1–2:15
2	Leading Others / Believing the Truth	1 Timothy 3:1–4:16	1 Timothy 3:1–4:16
3	Managing Relationships / Finding Contentment	1 Timothy 5:1–21; 6:6–19	1 Timothy 5:1–6:21
4	Strength in Suffering / Persevering in Christ	2 Timothy 1:1–2:13	2 Timothy 1:1–2:13
5	Workers Pleasing to God / Following the Truth	2 Timothy 2:14–3:17	2 Timothy 2:14–4:22
6	Role Models / Life in the Spirit	Titus 2:1–3:15	Titus 1:1–3:15

Generally, the ideal size you will want for the group is between eight to ten people, which ensures everyone will have enough time to participate in discussions. If you have more people, you might want to break up the main group into smaller subgroups. Encourage those who show up at the first meeting to commit to attending the duration of the study, as this will help the group members get to know each other, create stability for the group, and help you know how to prepare each week.

Each of the lessons begins with a brief reflection that highlights the theme you will be discussing that week. As you begin your group time, have the group members briefly respond to the opening question to get them thinking about the topic at hand. Some people may want to tell a long story in response to one of these questions, but the goal is to keep the answers brief. Ideally, you want everyone in the group to get a chance to answer, so try to keep the responses to just a few minutes. If you have more talkative group members, say up front that everyone needs to limit his or her answer to two minutes.

Give the group members a chance to answer, but tell them to feel free to pass if they wish. With the rest of the study, it's generally not a good idea to have everyone answer every question—a free-flowing discussion is more desirable. But with the opening reflection question, you can go around the circle. Encourage shy people to share, but don't force them.

Before your first meeting, let the group members know how the lessons are broken down. During your group discussion time the members will be drawing on the answers they wrote to the Exploration and Reaction sections, so encourage them to always complete these ahead of time. Also, invite them to bring any questions and insights they uncovered while reading to your next meeting, especially if they had a breakthrough moment or if they didn't understand something they read.

WEEKLY PREPARATION

As the leader, there are a few things you should do to prepare for each meeting:

- *Read through the lesson.* This will help you to become familiar with the content and know how to structure the discussion times.
- *Decide which questions you want to discuss.* Depending on how you structure your group time, you may not be able to cover every question. So select the questions ahead of time that you absolutely want the group to explore.
- *Be familiar with the questions you want to discuss.* When the group meets you'll be watching the clock, so you want to make sure you are familiar with the Bible study questions you have selected. You can then spend time in the passage again when the group meets. In this way, you'll ensure you have the passage more deeply in your mind than your group members.
- *Pray for your group.* Pray for your group members throughout the week and ask God to lead them as they study his Word.
- *Bring extra supplies to your meeting.* The members should bring their own pens for writing notes, but it's a good idea to have extras available for those who forget. You may also want to bring paper and additional Bibles.

Note that in many cases there will not be one "right" answer to the question. Answers will vary, especially when the group members are being asked to share their personal experiences.

STRUCTURING THE DISCUSSION TIME

You will need to determine with your group how long you want to meet each week so you can plan your time accordingly. Generally, most groups like to meet for either sixty minutes or ninety minutes, so you could use one of the following schedules:

Section	60 Minutes	90 Minutes
WELCOME (members arrive and get settled)	5 minutes	10 minutes
REFLECTION (discuss the opening question for the lesson)	10 minutes	15 minutes
DISCUSSION (discuss the Bible study questions in the Exploration and Reaction sections)	35 minutes	50 minutes
PRAYER/CLOSING (pray together as a group and dismiss)	10 minutes	15 minutes

As the group leader, it is up to you to keep track of the time and keep things moving along according to your schedule. You might want to set a timer for each segment so both you and the group members know when your time is up. (Note that there are some good phone apps for timers that play a gentle chime or other pleasant sound instead of a disruptive noise.) Don't feel pressured to cover every question you have selected if the group has a good discussion going. Again, it's not necessary to go around the circle and make everyone share.

Don't be concerned if the group members are silent or slow to share. People are often quiet when they are pulling together their ideas, and this might be a new experience for them. Just ask a question and let it hang in the air until someone shares. You can then say, "Thank you. What about others? What came to you when you reflected on the passage?"

GROUP DYNAMICS

Leading a group through *Life Lessons from 1 and 2 Timothy and Titus* will prove to be highly rewarding both to you and your group members—but that doesn't mean you will not encounter any challenges along the way! Discussions can get off track. Group members may not be sensitive to the needs and ideas of others. Some might worry they will be expected to talk about matters that make them feel awkward. Others may express comments that result in disagreements. To help ease this strain on you and the group, consider the following ground rules:

- When someone raises a question or comment that is off the main topic, suggest you deal with it another time, or, if you feel led to go in that direction, let the group know you will be spending some time discussing it.
- If someone asks a question you don't know how to answer, admit it and move on. At your discretion, feel free to invite group members to comment on questions that call for personal experience.
- If you find one or two people are dominating the discussion time, direct a few questions to others in the group. Outside the main group time, ask the more dominating members to help you draw out the quieter ones. Work to make them a part of the solution instead of the problem.
- When a disagreement occurs, encourage the group members to process the matter in love. Encourage those on opposite sides to restate what they heard the other side say about the matter, and then invite each side to evaluate if that perception is accurate. Lead the group in examining other Scriptures related to the topic and look for common ground.

When any of these issues arise, encourage your group members to follow the words from the Bible: "Love one another" (John 13:34), "If it is possible, as far as it depends on you, live at peace with everyone" (Romans 12:18), and, "Be quick to listen, slow to speak and slow to become angry" (James 1:19).

Thank you again for taking the time to lead your group. May God reward your efforts and dedication and make your time together in this study fruitful for his kingdom.

ALSO AVAILABLE IN THE LIFE LESSONS SERIES

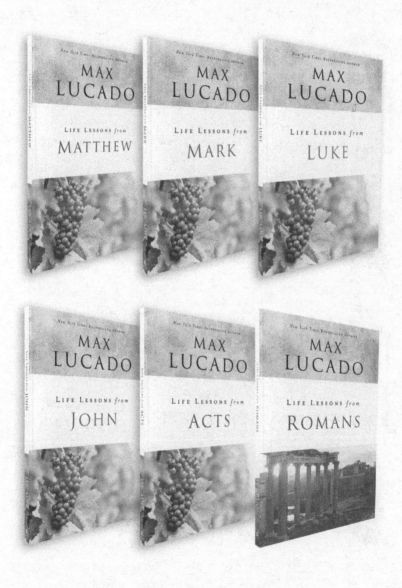

Now available wherever books and ebooks are sold.

ALSO AVAILABLE IN THE LIFE LESSONS SERIES

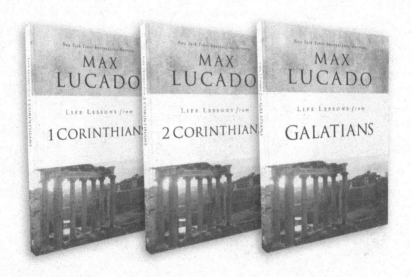

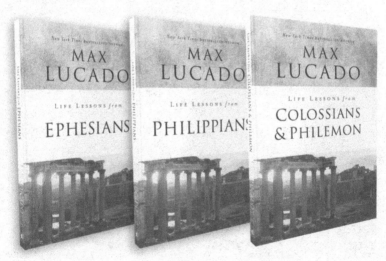

*Now available wherever books
and ebooks are sold.*